MASTERS OF
MONEY

KC ROTTOK CHESAINA

JONATHAN BALL PUBLISHERS
JOHANNESBURG, CAPE TOWN & LONDON

Originally published in South Africa in 2022 by
JONATHAN BALL PUBLISHERS
A division of Media24 (Pty) Ltd
PO Box 33977
Jeppestown
2043

ISBN 978-1-77619-157-4
ebook ISBN 978-1-77619-158-1

Every effort has been made to trace the copyright holders and to obtain their permission for the use of copyright material. The publishers apologise for any errors or omissions and would be grateful to be notified of any corrections that should be incorporated in future editions of this book.

www.jonathanball.co.za
Twitter: www.twitter.com/JonathanBallPub
Facebook: www.facebook.com/JonathanBallPublishers

Cover by Sean Robertson
Design and typesetting by Martine Barker
Set in Metropolis/Adobe Garamond Pro

CONTENTS

To she who nurtured my literature,
Ciarunji, my mother.

And she who captured my imagination,
Mueni, my wife.

FOREWORD

A key component of learning to navigate life is to have role models who set examples and – if we are very lucky – mentor us. I have been immensely lucky in my career to have many mentors. My passion, away from running the biggest and oldest stock exchange in Africa, is summiting mountains and scaling rockfaces. In many ways both of my passions are a metaphor for life; you don't know what you will meet on the trail, or how you will react; all you can do is prepare the best you can.

Critically, those who are determined to summit and get to the top know that choosing the right guide is as critical as investing in the right equipment. Guides are often not just literal leaders but also incredible sources of wisdom, who become role models for those wishing to pursue their sport at the highest altitude and in the most adverse conditions imaginable. The higher we climb, the greater our responsibilities, so we seek out those who can teach us more so that we can do what we love better, more safely and with greater success.

When South Africa entered the COVID-19 lockdown in March 2020 as the globe began to grapple with the worst public health crisis in living memory, there was no playbook for what we were about to do. I sought solace in the words and wisdom of the father of the modern South African nation, Nelson Mandela, as I began to understand how he had successfully summitted the mountains that life – and a repressive regime – had placed in his way.

The world of business, and the new normal that bobs in its wake, is daunting even to those who command boardroom tables. Leadership is never easy and it is even more challenging in such times.

For those who succeed without access to privilege, people who might look different, worship different gods, speak other languages, it sometimes seems an almost impossible task to scale those boardroom heights. But scale them we must because business should reflect the broader communities it serves. We must transform business – from the way it is run to the demographics of those who staff and lead it all the way through to the very people who benefit from its success.

If the pandemic has shown us anything, it has revealed just how inequality fragments the world. Especially in our beloved country, South Africa, inequality is rampant. As we start to build back better, as we must, to ensure that our businesses are more resilient in ever more trying times, we must ensure that the work those businesses do and the benefits they produce help to create sustainable communities where poverty and hunger soon become a thing of the past.

The first step on this journey is to find guides or mentors who can help us to find the way. This is why I am delighted to have been asked to write this foreword to KC Rottok Chesaina's *Masters of Money*, a collection of interviews with chief financial officers of some of the country's biggest companies. This book not only recognises individuals for their achievements but also helps us to learn from them.

A common thread that runs through this collection is not luck, as the cynics might have expected, but rather the persistence and consistency of those who are featured. It is a truism of life that you must show up every day, come rain or shine. Even if it's sometimes the hardest thing to do, when you are on the trail you have to keep climbing.

Another telling revelation is that life journeys are often not linear, but organic. Sometime the road less travelled, the one which seems to go off on a sidetrack, is precisely the road we ought to take. Those of us who are brave – or foolhardy – enough to reject common wisdom and go on exactly this road are more often than not incredibly well rewarded for our faith in the journey.

It's fitting that KC has chosen to focus on chief financial officers, since they play an absolutely vital role in any company by keeping one eye on the income statement and another on the balance sheet. Neglecting to do so can be as potentially catastrophic as ignoring the build-up

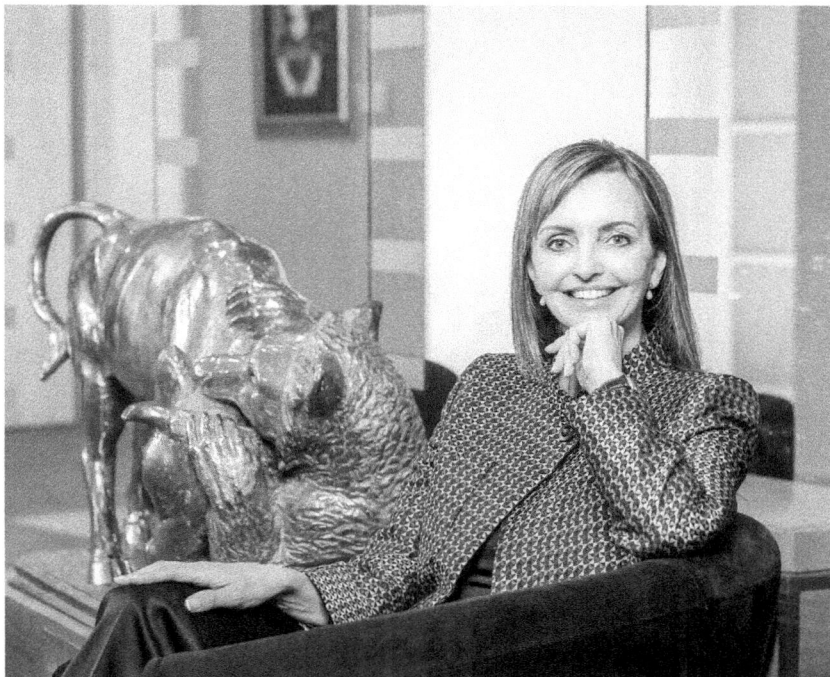

JSE Group CEO Dr Leila Fourie *(Photo: Devin Lester)*

of clouds and the passage of the sun as you make your way inch by inch up the sheer rock face.

There are many reasons for buying this book – to satisfy your curiosity, to be inspired and to learn. This is where you will find the answers to your questions about how to be a finance leader and a successful Master of Money in today's world. And, as you travel along the trails of life on the way to the summit of your own success, be sure to honour those who have gone before you.

Dr Leila Fourie
Group Chief Executive Officer
Johannesburg Stock Exchange

Old Mutual's Casper Troskie *(Photo: Debbie Yazbek)*

CASPER TROSKIE

A leader, not a manager

— INTERVIEW: FEBRUARY 2021 —

It's not every CFO who causes ripples on the bourse. But when Casper Troskie decided to leave Liberty for Old Mutual, the news of his resignation resulted in a change of half a billion rand in Liberty's market capitalisation on the Johannesburg Stock Exchange (JSE) in early January 2018. It is testimony to the market's perception of Casper having been a pillar of stability at Liberty.

Old Mutual was actually his very first client when he was a young audit clerk at Deloitte in Cape Town, Casper tells me, smiling in a way that recruits both his cheeks and eyes. He exudes warmth and approach-ability, despite, according to his own description, being an introvert.

His journey to an executive finance position began with choosing to become a chartered accountant (CA). 'My father encouraged me to become a CA. He founded the department of mathematical statistics at the University of Cape Town (UCT) in 1964 and played a role in the development of many actuaries, including my boss, Old Mutual CEO Iain Williamson. With a strong domestic background in numerical studies, I slid comfortably into pursuing a Bachelor of Commerce degree at UCT, graduating with an honours degree in 1987.'

After his studies, Casper joined Deloitte for articles and was later appointed to the role of audit manager. In 1996, he met Arnold Shapiro,

CEO of Capital Alliance Asset Managers, who was looking for a CFO for his business.

'I was very wet behind the ears!' Casper laughs. 'Imagine – at the age of 33 – going from audit to becoming a CFO. It was a steep learning curve.'

The stint was brief, as Casper joined Ohlthaver & List (O&L) just a couple of years later. The Namibia-based group had a majority stake in Namibia Breweries, among other business interests, including being franchise holder for Pick n Pay supermarkets in Namibia, a fishing joint venture, farms and game reserves.

'It was a very complex business, with a lot of debt on its balance sheet. Soon after I joined, interest rates went through the roof and we had to restructure the business, which involved selling 25% of our stake in Namibia Breweries to Becks. The transaction was very demanding and when it was done, I decided it was time for a change and rejoined Deloitte in Durban.'

At Deloitte, Casper was appointed head of the financial services business, with the Board of Executors (BoE), Marriott and McCarthy Insurance as some of his big clients. In 2003, a run on BoE led to its merging with Nedbank.

'The merger significantly reduced my client portfolio and I decided to move to Johannesburg, where I was appointed lead partner for the Nedbank audit. I joined in the year the bank needed to do a massive (R5 billion) rights issue and my involvement in doing the advisory work on that transaction required long hours. I learnt a lot, but it was quite stressful.'

Casper progressed within Deloitte to become the national head of the financial services audit division, which was also responsible for the actuarial function. In 2008, however, the world of commerce beckoned again and he joined Standard Bank as CFO, reporting to the financial director. He was enrolled into the bank's executive committee the following year.

'My appointment coincided with the global financial crisis, which was quite nerve-wracking. It was a significant challenge I had to deal with, yet I had just come from an audit background and had to get to grips with banking quite quickly. There was a global shortage of liquidity and a credit crunch. The bank had also gone on an expansion drive into

Europe, South America and the rest of Africa. We had to work day and night to keep so many balls in the air.'

Two years later, having amassed some banking experience, Casper was asked to apply for the CFO role at Liberty Holdings, a subsidiary of Standard Bank, and was appointed to the role in October 2010. Among the executives he engaged with was Peter Moyo, who was then a board member of Liberty.

When Moyo was appointed CEO of Old Mutual Emerging Markets in 2017, he approached Casper to take up the CFO role. 'It was a hard decision to make, but ultimately I decided to take up the offer and be part of listing the company. The announcement was made in January 2018 and I joined officially in March after the lapse of my mandatory gardening leave. After prelisting roadshows around the world, Old Mutual Limited was listed on the JSE in 2018.'

Casper has faced many challenges since joining Old Mutual, including having to dispose of the business interest in Latin America and dealing with inflation and the currency crisis in Zimbabwe, which have had an adverse effect on the company there. 'There was also the much-publicised spat between Old Mutual and Peter Moyo, which caused a lot of uncertainty. It was stressful.'

Moyo was suspended in May 2019 and dismissed from his position as CEO. He fought the dismissal in a drawn-out legal battle that lasted close to a year, with the courts eventually ruling in Old Mutual's favour. The ruling ended the uncertainty around who Casper would work with in the role of CEO. Casper does not expand further on this thorny issue, other than noting that he ended up being 'caught in the middle'.

DEALING WITH CHALLENGES

Casper's been in important positions that came with big responsibility and many challenges for most of his career. I ask him what his advice is for other professionals facing a crisis.

'Often you feel like you cannot divorce yourself from the problem. You feel personally responsible, even if you're not, and that's what causes stress. I therefore advise professionals not to take to heart difficulties that are not of their own making.

'There are some things I simply do not have control over. I cannot influence how many people will pass away from COVID. I need to be clear about what I can manage and set goals to achieve them.'

He reveals that Old Mutual does a lot of scenario analysis and stress testing to help it project the possibility of adverse events and subsequently prepare for them.

'The key here is preparation. Before the COVID-19 crisis hit, we had already put in place certain structures to mitigate its impact. We run our shareholder funds in a collar structure, where we manage our returns within a corridor. This means you are protected when you have a crisis. You have to think about that beforehand, so that when a crisis hits you're able to pull the right levers and derisk your balance sheet.'

No one could have foreseen the extent of the pandemic. But, he says, 'even when the unexpected happens, having some level of preparation enables you to stay calm and think around what actions to take, with a sober, level-headed mindset. It is also important to have experienced colleagues in this regard; I really admire our chief risk officer, Richard Treagus, whose work has enabled the group to be resilient in the current turbulence.'

Our conversation started with him apologising for being a few minutes late after a check-in conversation with a colleague had gone over time. His account offers insight into what makes him such a respected leader.

'In these COVID times you cannot be transactional when you host meetings with your team. A meeting with any team member has to begin with finding out how they're doing, which informs how you should approach your engagement going forward.'

Casper's colleague appeared healthy, but only when Casper probed further did he find out his team member had recently been discharged from hospital after having been on a ventilator battling COVID.

'We've had to change our culture and improve on our engagement with staff members and clients. With almost all our staff working from home, we need to have frequent sessions to talk to each other and let people know they are not alone. By having these chats, we identify where people are struggling and determine how we can help them cope.'

With a large force of advisers being unable to service clients during the pandemic, Old Mutual could have saved on fees, but the group decided to continue supporting them financially. 'We're taking the long-term view and relying on our strong balance sheet to support our people during this time. Furthermore, we are investing in capacitating all our staff to continue to work remotely.

'And given that we are in the insurance business, we of course have to deal with the results of the pandemic. We've reacted quite quickly in honouring the life and funeral cover claims that have been the consequence of the disease.'

LEADERSHIP AND MENTORSHIP

For Casper, true leadership means giving employees appropriate guidance to do their jobs properly yet affording them freedom in their roles. 'Be a leader rather than a manager. Once you have assessed your people's ability [for] their roles, you need to trust them to execute the strategy.'

Casper oversees numerous functions at Old Mutual, including company secretarial, investor relations, taxation, actuarial services and the legal department. 'I have neither the time nor the ability to perform all these functions and hence I need to ensure that I'm comfortable with the person leading each team,' he says.

'I am no legal expert, for example, so my role is to ensure that I have the right person in charge of that division. I've been told that I'm a very goal-oriented person, who can be intimidating. At the same time, I think I am approachable … I think you need to have the appropriate balance to implement strategies while demonstrating that you care for people and their development.'

Casper won several Partner Awards while at Deloitte and was a finalist for the South African CFO of the Year in 2015. Not having a family background in business, he has relied on mentors taking a personal interest in his career, such as Philip Wessels, his first manager at Deloitte, Richard Dunn, then COO at Deloitte, and the late Vassi Naidoo, CEO at the audit firm at the time.

As a way of paying it forward, Casper always has about seven mentees who he makes time for. Some of them have gone on to hold quite senior positions, including his successor at Liberty, Yuresh Maharaj, and Smangaliso Mkhabela, founder of The Shard, a boutique actuarial and analytical consultancy.

According to Casper another vital responsibility of a good leader is to set strategies and ensure they are implemented. 'Strategy is all about execution. You can have a good strategy, but if you cannot execute it then it becomes meaningless. The strategy must also be inspirational; people need to be moved by the strategy to give it their all. It should also be customer focused because if you don't have a customer, you do not have a business.'

He says a strategy needs to have a long-term view and progress must be measured at appropriate intervals, also considering current trends in the industry. 'For instance, in our business, convergence has led to many different platform businesses becoming our competitors. Amazon may have started selling books online but before you knew it, they developed a platform to sell insurance. So, our competitors are not necessarily people in financial services. You need to anticipate such trends to develop a strategy that is bulletproof.'

Another aspect of Casper's strategy playbook is information gathering. According to him research is critical to ensure that decisions are made from a point of knowledge.

LESSONS LEARNT AND FUTURE PLANS

Casper is a father of three. The eldest, Joshua, lives in New Zealand, and the two younger children, Casper and Natasja, are both Bachelor of Commerce students in Cape Town. I asked him what advice he would give them as they prepare for the professional world. Put differently, what advice would he give his 25-year-old self?

'Joshua actually is 25! He started a DJ company with the son of the New Zealand prime minister.' He chuckles, 'I'm not sure what advice I could give him seeing that, unlike me, he is a total extrovert!

'Anyway, the one mistake I think I made was staying in auditing for too long. I definitely should have gone into commerce much earlier and stayed there.'

Still, Casper did learn important life lessons from his experience in auditing. 'In Durban, I was part of some really problematic audits. I learnt that if you're not comfortable with something, do not accept it. If there's something that you're unable to live with morally, you need to make yourself heard as soon as possible.

'Trust your gut and do not procrastinate. Don't worry too much about whose feathers you may end up ruffling. If you're wrong, you can apologise later. But trust your gut.'

He advises dealing with problems as quickly as possible. 'Do not put off to tomorrow what you can do today. Even while I am on holiday, I make sure I clear my inbox daily. It's an important discipline to have, because if you deal with issues promptly, they don't build up into bigger problems later.'

At this point Casper sits up. 'Integrity! Integrity! Integrity!' he says animatedly. 'You *must* have integrity to be successful. Think about it: I deal with a very large board; there are 250 people reporting to me directly and the group has 28 000 employees. If there's an inconsistency in the way you operate, people will see through it. You must have strong values and put the goals of the group ahead of your own agenda.'

Looking to the future, Casper plans on transforming the finance function at Old Mutual by modernising the company's systems and putting their finance infrastructure on the cloud.

In the next two to three years, he also needs to find a successor and then 'will probably occupy a few board seats as a non-executive director. I don't think I will go straight into retirement; that would be like a vehicle that's been going at 100 miles an hour coming to a sudden and complete stop.'

When I ask him if he fancies becoming a CEO, he pauses for a moment. 'No. I'm very clear on what value I add and on my expertise. In November [2020], we successfully raised a bond of R2 billion at good pricing in the middle of a pandemic. Things like that are the things I find exciting and what I enjoy doing. That's what I'm good at.'

DINEO MOLEFE

The purpose-driven mentality

— INTERVIEW: JULY 2021 —

Dineo Molefe is guided by values – whether in her career or her personal life. 'Once we have scaled the corporate heights, made the money we were to make and held the positions we wanted to hold, it will all boil down to whether we've made a difference to humanity or not,' says the CFO of telecommunications giant MTN South Africa. 'That's what's important; that's what we should keep in mind in all our endeavours.'

Dineo grew up in Diepkloof, Soweto, in an all-female household. Her grandmother was a tea lady at a bank, her mother a seamstress. Together the pair raised Dineo and her sisters in a home that valued the importance of education. The absence of men meant that there was no patriarchal dominance that could smother her desire to pursue a corporate career, as happened in many households in the township at the time.

In high school, Dineo loved accounting – and she was quite good at it – which made her choice of a degree course fairly simple when she enrolled at the University of South Africa in 1994. She graduated with an honours degree in accounting in 1999 and joined Grant Thornton Johannesburg for a training contract – a requirement to qualify as a chartered accountant (CA). Given that she had to work while studying to pay her course fees, Dineo considers meeting all the requirements

MTN's Dineo Molefe *(Photo: Phillip Erasmus)*

to qualify as a CA one of the greatest achievements of her life.

At the start of her career, Dineo moved around a lot, setting clear targets for herself and learning as much as she could at each institution. She joined Gobodo in 2000, where she worked as an audit supervisor for a year before moving to the Industrial Development Corporation as a senior internal auditor. She was appointed as a senior financial adviser at Eskom in 2004, a position she held until 2006 when she joined Sizwe Ntsaluba VSP (today SNG Grant Thornton) for a brief stint as a senior manager.

In 2007, Dineo joined the Thebe Investment Corporation, a group of companies with interests in multiple sectors, including petrochemicals, infrastructure, tourism, media and agriculture. She worked as group financial manager for two years before being promoted to group finance director in April 2010.

'Whenever I join an organisation, I determine what I want to achieve there,' Dineo says. 'Once I accomplish my targets, I count it as a highlight and move on. At Thebe, I wanted to establish finance as an integral part of the cycle rather than a function that was only called upon at the tail end when reporting was required.'

She is passionate about helping people grow their careers and has been involved in several projects to this end almost from the start of her career, constantly thinking about how she can help team members progress. Today, 20 years after starting out on her own career journey, she still finds it hard to say no to people who approach her for mentorship help, even if they are virtual strangers who connect via a professional network platform such as LinkedIn. She believes it is her way of paying it forward.

According to Hlobisile Mtshali, who worked as an accountant at Thebe when Dineo was the CFO, Dineo is the kind of leader who takes pride in the accomplishments of those she empowers and 'believes in her team members more than they believe in themselves'.

'There was this one time when our group financial manager fell ill a week before we had to present to the Audit Committee,' Hlobisile recalls. 'Dineo told me that since we'd come so far, the show had to go on. Despite me having no experience at that level, she entrusted me with delivering the tax status report to the committee, saying there was no time like the present to learn. She gave me constructive feedback after my presentation and invited me to tag along to board meetings of a listed entity that she chaired.'

In July 2014, Dineo left Thebe to join the telecommunications company Vodacom as a finance executive. Here her role entailed financial planning and analysis, which she didn't find as stimulating as she had hoped, and consequently she spent just under two years at the company.

T-SYSTEMS SOUTH AFRICA AND EMPOWERING WOMEN

In May 2016, Dineo accepted an offer to join T-Systems South Africa (TSSA) as CFO. The company was a subsidiary of Deutsche Telekom, an ICT (information and communications technology) services company with clients in both the public and private sectors.

While at Thebe, she established a women's empowerment programme called *Thebe Ya Mosadi*. Her drive for mentorship and female empowerment continued at T-Systems, where she led the *Women of T-Systems* initiative. Being involved in these initiatives stems from her desire to help women gain the necessary skills to foster leadership and overcome behaviours that stunt their professional growth.

'I'm extremely proud of what has been achieved by these two initiatives,' says Dineo. 'They've helped uplift women, who, in turn, are passing on the lessons learnt to their own daughters and communities. Despite equal opportunities, the ability to fully exercise those opportunities differs between men and women. Being a mother is a wonderful part of womanhood, but it comes with unique pressures that men do not face as they build their careers, because taking care of children predominantly lies with mothers.'

After two years as CFO, Dineo was promoted to managing director of TSSA. Having held finance roles previously, this was a new challenge as she was charged with repositioning the business for growth and sustainability. But drawing on what she had learnt in the Advanced Management Program at the University of Pennsylvania's Wharton School in 2012 helped.

The role involved shifting TSSA's market focus to increase the company's efficiency and customer base while navigating the business through a number of critical issues. Her efforts in reconfiguring the business bore fruit: it became an attractive proposition to potential buyers and in late 2020, the ICT company Gijima announced its impending acquisition of TSSA.

'My plan was to take time off from a permanent role after the sale of TSSA, and only serve in the non-executive director positions I had at Thebe and the Spur Group,' Dineo reveals. 'But when MTN approached me about the CFO position for the South African operations, I simply had to consider it. I found it a very attractive prospect to join a giant Pan-African organisation, which, at its heart, has the agenda of fostering the economic growth of the continent and serving its people.'

JOINING MTN AND CRAFTING STRATEGY

Dineo joined the telecommunications provider MTN in November 2020, at the start of South Africa's second COVID-19 wave. From a business perspective, the pandemic resulted in huge demand for connectivity, which boosted data sales. But with everyone working from home, she got to meet physically with her full team only several months later.

'Joining a company during a pandemic is a barrier to our engagement because it prevents optimum relationship building. In addition, many of our colleagues were ill and some passed away because of COVID-related complications. I also tested positive in early 2021. It wasn't a pleasant experience, and after I recovered it took me a couple of months to regain my normal energy levels.'

The CFO role in MTN is fairly operational. As such, Dineo is involved in the mechanics of running the business. 'At a senior level, you shape your role. You need to determine what your role will be in the organisation according to what interests you and how you think your talents can better the company. I don't position myself in MTN as responsible for only the finance function; I lead with a mindset that I am jointly responsible for the success or failure of the entire organisation.'

Given that everything the business does boils down to rands and cents, finance's influence is spread across the entire entity. Therefore, as the company's chief finance leader, Dineo is an integral part of the strategic and operational direction of the business. According to her, clarity is one of the most important elements of a successful strategy.

'It is important to be clear about what it is that you will do, and what you will not do. Without that, we run the risk of people trying to do everything. And there needs to be a common understanding of the dependencies: those that are overt and those that are hidden. The hidden dependencies require discernment, as they can lead to a failure in the strategy if they go unchecked.'

Having a pragmatic execution plan is also fundamental to the success of an organisation's strategy, Dineo believes. This includes identifying the right people in the right positions to execute the plan, and not being afraid to experiment before fully embarking on the steps laid out in the plan. And, she says, once the strategy is running, you must be flexible enough to adapt the plan's execution depending on what you discover and learn along the journey.

HANDLING CRISIS AND ADVICE FOR PROFESSIONALS

If she could do it all over again, Dineo says she would allocate less time to work than she did at the start of her career. She advises young professionals to be less hurried. 'It seems as if we are all under extreme pressure that everything needs to happen now. It is important to regularly take time to pause and evaluate whether what we're doing is aligned to what we were put on earth to do.'

Dineo firmly believes that we all have a life purpose and that professionals need to assess whether what they are doing is fulfilling that purpose and aligned to their values. One should be guided by what brings one inner peace, rather than doing things that please other.

'When going down a particular road in your career, have regular check-ins with yourself to see if what you are doing contributes to your peace and joy. Take time to evaluate whether it contributes to your wellness – spiritual and otherwise. Set clear boundaries for yourself, which you will not cross regardless of how financially rewarding it may be. For example, don't take up a job at an organisation whose activities are not aligned with your values.'

Dineo also believes professionals should apply themselves fully rather than worry about what they are not doing at that particular moment. If you are at work, give yourself fully to your work, and likewise when you are at home. Do not try to do everything at the same time – understand who you are as a person and be true to who you are.

'So, for example, I see myself as a woman whose life's purpose is to make a positive contribution to all those around her. I'm positioned to uplift and contribute to people's growth and success using whatever means are available to me. I've been graced with many gifts, including the gift of life and a keen interest in the advancement of women.'

In becoming who she is, Dineo has faced many challenges. Having grown up in abject poverty, where something like having meat in a meal was a luxury, she stresses the importance of gratitude to her own children, and repeatedly nudges them to be considerate of the less fortunate. Once, when the family was driving through Johannesburg, they saw a homeless boy walking barefoot along the side of the road. There and then she ordered one of her sons to give the boy his shoes. She is nurturing her children to be givers and to appreciate everything they have as a product of hard work rather than something they are entitled to.

Losing her husband in her twenties was devastating. 'My life has seen a number of crises, including bereavement and stressful work situations,' Dineo says. 'I handle these circumstances by focusing on the end goal and seeing everything that happens in between as part of the process. Nothing that's worth doing is easy and I've developed resilience from the tough experiences I had to endure.'

Dineo classifies crises into three types: those that happen as a consequence of our actions; those that happen to us despite our actions; and those, like the COVID-19 pandemic, that happen to the entire human race. She believes that in all three cases, we are given what we have the capacity to handle. She believes that remaining steadfast in pursuing your life's purpose will give you the necessary strength to deal with challenges.

'There is no endless night ... eventually morning comes,' declares Dineo. 'You should just recognise that life is full of seasons – gloomy winters and sunny summers. It is important to recognise which season you're in and to adapt to what's required of you in that particular season.'

Dineo takes from various sources to guide how she lives her life. The

Bible is her favourite book, giving her the appropriate guidance for her decisions. She also reads other books and applies whatever noble teachings they may have – as long as they do not conflict with the Good Book. One she recommends is *The Book of Joy* by the Dalai Lama and Desmond Tutu.

'The authors reflect on the journey of life and what is important. They cover what really gives joy and meaning to life and what should and should not move you as an individual. This book helps you reflect on where your focus should be and reminds you that you need to choose your battles.'

It is thanks to strong values, a clear sense of purpose and incredible integrity that Dineo moves forward each day and is able to tackle not only her work but also every interaction beyond the office.

HARRY KELLAN

Finance leader of Africa's largest bank

— INTERVIEW: MARCH 2021 —

Given that he does so few media interviews, Harry Kellan is somewhat of a mystery. But the folk who know him well have the highest regard for his focus and work ethic. He is a leader who is always looking for opportunities to share his knowledge – but don't ask an introvert to talk about himself!

'I hope this interview is not going to be about building my profile,' is his opening line as we settle down to chat. 'I always decline invitations for interviews because I see myself as having a job to do which I need to focus on. I don't have the time to push a personal profile or agenda. I accepted the opportunity to speak to you because your project appears to be geared toward educating upcoming professionals; a noble objective which I'm happy to take part in,' Harry says as he swivels in his chair.

WHEN HARRY MET COUNTING

Harry would have spent a lot of time behind swivel chairs if he had stuck to the family tradition, with his father and both grandfathers having been barbers.

'I have my mother to thank for placing a premium on education. She was a teacher and we grew up with a strong focus on education. In those days, Indian families thought highly of the medical profession

FirstRand's Harry Kellan *(Photo: Cindy Ellis)*

and in keeping with that perception I initially opted for medicine and pharmacy as my first two choices at university. I was unable to get into either course and had to settle for my third choice, a bachelor's degree in science.'

What was supposed to be a route to eventually fulfilling the dream of becoming a doctor turned out to be a nightmare. He struggled with subjects such as biology, chemistry and physics, which were essential subjects in the first year of science, let alone the struggle with the transition to university study. The only subject he seemed to excel at was mathematics.

'I could choose to keep on the path of least resistance and continue trying to become a doctor, or change to a different degree. I chose the latter and it was not easy. It meant accepting failure, disappointing my parents and facing the financial cost of a wasted academic year.'

Harry's father was unimpressed and informed him that he would subsequently get money only for 'running costs'.

'To many European families, becoming a chartered accountant is as big an achievement as becoming a doctor. In an Indian family back then, and likely still a little today, it is a very big step down.'

Harry pursued a Bachelor of Commerce degree at the University of the Witwatersrand, completing his honours degree in financial accounting in 1994. He had to depend on loans and bursaries to pay for his studies and he also did, as he says, 'a lot' of vacation work at various accounting firms – to cover costs, yes, but more so to line up options for his articles.

ARTHUR ANDERSEN AND HSBC

Despite being in the top ten per cent of his class, he was unable to get vacation work at the big audit firms.

'It was just before the end of apartheid and the big audit firms didn't have large intakes of students of colour to pursue training contracts. At the time, I thought it was a race thing, but over time I've come to appreciate that it was more than that. I'm an introvert and grew up in a culture where children were to be seen and not heard. You can have good qualifications, but the way you present yourself in interviews may not convince the panel that you'll make a good hire.'

Harry says that effective communication is a vital skill for any professional. 'It's an important part of my job; communicating with my finance teams, my peers at executive level, the board, fellow directors, and our many stakeholders.

'Good communicators force themselves to stop and listen. Like right now, in our discourse, I need to be able to pause and really try to understand your objective for our discussion, so that when I speak, I stick to the objective rather than just telling a story for the sake of telling it. Relevance is crucial.'

He joined Arthur Andersen for articles in 1995. It was the smallest of the then Big Five audit firms, and he thought it a good choice because he was under the impression that it would be easier to stand out in a smaller organisation. 'That was not really true, because even big ponds are made up of many small ones. Another drawcard was the training in Eindhoven in the Netherlands, my first time out of the country – and if I'm completely honest, that was the real decider!'

Harry was deployed to financial services audits and after three years of articles, he was seconded to the London office of the international firm.

'It was my first trip to the United Kingdom. I flew out on a Friday, arrived at Heathrow on a Saturday and on the Monday I was at the Merrill Lynch office to report for duty. After twelve months, I was appointed manager and attended the [Arthur Andersen] manager school at St Charles in Illinois in the USA.'

Harry and his wife decided that Britain was not where they wanted to raise their family, and they returned to South Africa, where he continued his career at Arthur Andersen's Johannesburg office.

Realising that auditing was not his cup of tea, he joined HSBC in Johannesburg in the Corporate Finance division in September 2000. 'At HSBC, I figured out quite quickly that I didn't want to become a career investment banker despite really enjoying the work. But the role expanded my problem-solving skills as I was exposed to real business issues, strategy and solutioning. A good example of that was when we were working on a financial model for a telecommunications operator. I learnt that no matter how large or complex the problem, you are only able to solve it by breaking it down into small, manageable chunks. By dissecting it into different components, we were able to develop a successful model.'

ONE OF THE YOUNGEST CFOS OF A MAJOR RETAIL BANK

After four years at HSBC, Harry began looking for a different opportunity in the financial services sector. Alan Hedding, the then CFO of First National Bank (FNB), was looking for a Head of Finance. Upon seeing Harry's CV, he invited him for a chat.

'Alan was previously a partner at Arthur Andersen, and he knew of me even though we didn't work together much at the audit firm. Without Alan I would not be where I am today. An important objective for young professionals to note is that wherever you find yourselves right now, you are creating a pipeline to the future. You are either building bridges or burning them.'

When Harry joined FNB in 2005, a number of people reporting to him were older and more experienced than he was. 'I had to rewire my brain to the idea that age does not matter and that everyone has the right to say something. I also took the time to convince my colleagues that they were working *with* me, not *for* me.'

He was offered the position of CFO at FNB (part of the FirstRand group) two years later. At only 35, Harry was apprehensive about the prospect of heading up the finance operations of one of South Africa's largest financial institutions. He thought he should decline the offer and told Hedding that he did not feel ready.

Harry recalls Hedding's words to him: 'Alan convinced me to take up the position. He said that it was a good thing I was second-guessing the idea of taking up the role, because second-guessing yourself keeps you nimble and on your toes. After making the decision to take up the position, I felt a bit like a cat on a hot tin roof. The lesson I learnt here was not to go around telling people that you're not good enough, because if you keep doing so, they will eventually believe you. I would not have been offered the role if my predecessor and others didn't think that I was good and ready enough!'

Once again, the introvert quickly had to learn to speak up.

'Sitting on the Exco [executive committee] of FNB meant that I had a choice between limiting myself to being just the finance person or having insight into the bank's business, for which finance is a scoreboard. There were seasoned executives from different divisions on the Exco and I had to make my voice heard. At that level, few individuals have the time to find their feet and there are no second chances … you have to hit the ground running.

'I was excited at the prospect, because it was a role which promised to nurture my ability as a leader. That's important for any position you accept as a professional. If you walk into a role feeling that you have all the necessary qualities to fulfil that role, then that's not the right role for you. If a role doesn't grow you, then it means that you're either stagnant or going backwards. Always seek an opportunity to learn.'

Soon after Harry had taken up the role, the global financial crisis hit. It was a period of extreme uncertainty in financial markets and the banking industry. To an extent, the South African banking system was insulated from the crisis by strong exchange control regulations. However, the South African economy went into recession for the first time in 17 years, which directly impacted the performance of the banking sector.

'It was unbelievably tough because there was a sudden decline in credit quality in the big lending books of the banks, particularly in home and vehicle loans. I'm grateful for that period, because you learn the most in the hardest of times. I learnt not to go into crisis mode – where the only two options are fight or flight. It's better to press the pause button and reflect on the permutations in order to find the best long-term solution.'

FNB changed their business model to focus on their transactional relationship with customers, investing in innovation to develop different ways of meeting customer needs. They further adopted 'the first loss is best loss' philosophy by working with their distressed customers to dispose of their encumbered properties early enough to avoid even greater losses from increased debt.

'Yet, sometimes you think you've been through the worst, when it was really just preparing you for even harder times to come,' Harry reflects when I ask him about the impact of the COVID-19 pandemic.

'From an economic-profit-generation perspective, this is the first time since the global financial crisis that the group has produced a return on equity below the cost of equity, which represents an economic loss,' Harry wrote in his CFO report for the year ending June 2020.

'However, FirstRand still delivered normalised earnings of R17.3 billion and grew shareholder net asset value, so the business is in resilient shape despite the challenging environment.'

The bank has had to deal with multiple issues, including loss of revenue from lockdowns, defaults in loan balances, providing relief to customers and recognising higher provisions for expected losses in future.

'I think we've done extremely well in dealing with these issues. Although I've played my part as group CFO, credit must go to the wider leadership team for how well we have performed. Are there things we could have done differently? Sure. But even if we had done some things differently, I don't believe it would have changed the outcomes materially. We can be proud of the actions we took to respond to the negative effects of the pandemic.'

ON STRATEGY AND ACHIEVEMENTS

Given the success of FirstRand's strategy in handling the COVID-19 pandemic and the crisis that our country and economy are facing, I ask Harry what he considers to be at the core of their approach.

'The key part of a strategy is understanding what you're trying to achieve. Most people will express their need to achieve growth in earnings or a certain return profile. Those are certainly outcomes or measures of a strategy, but ultimately your strategy must align with your purpose as a business. So, if you say you're here to serve society or to address customer needs, that should be the core of the strategy from which you develop key performance indicators such as, for instance, earnings.'

Harry observes that many organisations make the mistake of changing strategy too often.

'For a strategy to be embedded, you can't change it every year. People try one thing and if it doesn't work, they decide to try something else. That's tactical. Strategy does not lend itself to tactics; it must be allowed the opportunity to live and its execution needs to exceed a mere year or two. You can tweak bits and pieces as you go along, but ultimately delivering on strategy is a long-term achievement.'

Taking part in formulating and implementing an effective strategy is a central part of Harry's position as group CFO of FirstRand. Given the size of the organisation, this role is a critical one.

The FirstRand group is the largest financial institution by market capitalisation on the African continent. It has a portfolio of integrated financial services businesses, including well-known local brands such as FNB, Wesbank, Rand Merchant Bank, Direct Axis and Ashburton Investments. It also has a challenger bank in the United Kingdom (Aldermore).

I ask Harry which appointment he considers his biggest achievement.

'Becoming a father three times over,' he declares without missing a beat. 'Our kids help me become a better person because I need to set a good example for them. As for professional achievements, my appointment to the group CFO role and FirstRand becoming Africa's largest bank by market capitalisation are certainly highlights. That said, we do not measure ourselves by the size of our market capitalisation, but by how well we deliver value to our shareholders and customers.'

In his engagement with employees, Harry has an open-door policy. 'Reporting lines are there for administrative purposes. But in reality people don't work for me, we work together. I'm a firm believer in the idea that if you work to build people, you build yourself. I also have the confidence to hire people that are smarter than me because I will learn from them and build a better team that way. We'll achieve our outcomes much more effectively with a smart team of individuals who have a common vision.'

LESSONS FOR YOUNG PROFESSIONALS

When it comes to lessons learnt so far, Harry advises career starters to embrace disappointments as their significance often becomes apparent only later.

'I was addressing trainee accountants last year and I used an extreme analogy to illustrate this lesson. Consider the question of who you wish to marry versus the person who you choose to marry. You may set out with the idea of marrying option A, like an A-list actress, but this option is only achievable by a select number of people. So, to achieve option B doesn't constitute failure and you should not view it as second best, because that option is likely to be the absolute best choice for you. The universe always has plans for you. Always.'

Harry further explains that he often sees job applicants who become very disappointed when they are turned down for the specific position, thinking that they are failures for not securing it. 'This is not always the right conclusion, because the process itself has meaning. By applying for a position in an organisation, especially an internal one, you make the decision-makers aware of your skill set, which may result in your securing a different position in the future – often better suited to you than the one you had applied for before.'

Another piece of advice Harry has for novices is patience. 'Youngsters of today view life as a fast-moving train that they need to jump on as quickly as possible to avoid being left behind. The ability to press pause is quite difficult for them! Darn, it is actually quite difficult for me! Even now that I'm on the brink of turning 50! But I have the ability now to remind myself from time to time to press pause, which is something I wasn't able to do as a 25-year-old.' Missing one train is not the be all and end all, he continues, because another train will come later, and the universe has multiple paths to success.

'The third piece of advice I would give a 25-year-old today is that they should understand that it's not all about them. Sometimes it is simply about luck ... being in the right place at the right time.

'Certainly, in my case, that is what happened. The lesson there is that the universe may open the doors of luck to you once or even twice. And when it does, you should be ready to seize the opportunity and produce the goods.'

There will always be opportunities to learn from, and entrants into the job market should embrace a willingness to grasp that which they didn't understand the day before.

'I'm not only talking about technical matters, but also the softer skills that come from everyday experiences. Young people should learn that it's okay to make mistakes. And it is perfectly fine to admit that you don't know something when asked. Do not assume that because you're being asked, you're expected to know the answer. Have the confidence to admit that you don't have the knowledge and afterwards be willing to retreat and research the answer.'

Harry concludes by sharing his recipe for a successful career starting small, always looking to improve and consistently fostering innovation.

BOTHWELL MAZARURA

Never walk alone

— INTERVIEW: MAY 2021 —

Murewa in the Mashonaland East province of rural Zimbabwe was somewhat of a paradise in the early 1970s. Acres and acres of endless land, enveloped by long, pale green grass, umbrella-shaped trees and the freshest air imaginable. This is where Bothwell Mazarura was born in 1973.

Each morning, his father, an agricultural officer, would wake up, jump on his motorcycle and ride out to visit farmers. There was something about his father, about farming and about making a living off the land that inspired Bothwell to pursue the career he has today. The notion of Africans thriving off the blessing of land, what is above it and what lies beneath, is the unerring nexus for farming and mining.

Bothwell's journey from 'plough and cow' to 'chuck it and truck it' entailed moving to the capital city, Harare, where his education journey took him to St George's College, a private Jesuit boys' high school. It was here that he heard about accounting as a profession and decided to apply for Deloitte's trainee programme. He joined the firm in 1993 and was subsequently deployed to a number of mining audits, including that of Anglo American's nickel operations in Zimbabwe.

At the same time, he pursued a distance-learning Bachelor of Accounting Science degree from the University of South Africa. After graduating, in 1996, he sat the board exams administered by the

Kumba Iron Ore's Bothwell Mazarura *(Photo: Adam Houghton Photography)*

Institute of Chartered Accountants of Zimbabwe. But for the first time in his budding career, he experienced a major disappointment: he failed the auditing section of the exam. He was driven to tears.

But the setback brought out Bothwell's dogged determination and inspired a formidable comeback. From an early age, his father had taught him to be committed and passionate about whatever he took on. And to never give up. Not only did he pass the rewrite, but he also rallied to fourth position in the country.

Upon qualifying as a chartered accountant in 1999, Bothwell was appointed a manager at Deloitte. He was seconded to the Nottingham office in the United Kingdom in 2000, which initially proved to be quite challenging. 'I experienced a culture shock. Going from rural Zimbabwe to living in Europe was such a stark contrast,' Bothwell says. 'The transition from a small country to a big pond was daunting, but I later realised the training I'd gone through up to that point had prepared me well to compete on a global scale.'

TRANSITION FROM AUDITING TO MINING

After two years in the UK, Bothwell returned to Harare and was appointed as partner at Deloitte Zimbabwe in June 2002, assuming executive responsibility for the human resources function of the firm. In a professional services practice, people are assets, and this role gave him a great vantage point from which to influence the strategic direction of the firm. After five years he moved to the Johannesburg office, but the change was not particularly smooth.

'In Harare, I was in a small office where I had a lot of strategic influence on how the firm was run. In Johannesburg, I was one of hundreds of partners and the organisation had an Exco [executive committee] who managed the firm. I struggled with the notion that I had very little say in the strategic direction of the firm.'

This was part of what nudged Bothwell to leave the audit firm and look for a space where he could make a difference. In August 2010, he joined the finance division of Lonmin, which, at the time, was listed on the London Stock Exchange and had platinum interests in the North West province.

The massacre of mineworkers at Lonmin's Marikana mine is an unforgettable blot on Bothwell's six-year stay at the company. On 16 August 2012, 34 miners were killed by members of the South African Police Service in a protracted strike in which miners were demanding a minimum wage of R12 500 per month.

'It was a defining moment for me to witness how the situation deteriorated so quickly and to observe the blunt reality of mining in South Africa,' he recalls. 'It was tempting to just walk away from the whole mess and free myself from the stress of the aftermath. But I realised that as Head of Finance, I had an opportunity to influence change, [something] that would have a positive impact on the lives of the miners and their families.'

Bothwell became a trustee of the provident fund set up for the employees and took part in the ensuing interaction with the unions. Following the fallout of the Marikana incident and the subsequent commodity down cycle, he participated in the efforts to save the company, which included two rights issues and two refinancing transactions.

The Marikana incident reinforced Bothwell's motivation for getting involved in mining in the first place, and the experience gained from the efforts to save the company would shape his both his personal and professional outlook later on.

In July 2016, he was head-hunted for the role of financial director at Wescoal. The prospect of being part of the growth story of a company that was majority black-owned and listed on the Johannesburg Stock Exchange was attractive.

'I was quite happy in my new role and I thought I'd be at Wescoal for many a year. But then Anglo American came calling. Given the long history I had with the company – going back to my clerk days in Zimbabwe – it was an opportunity I had to give serious consideration. My decision to take the leap was informed by my conviction that I'd be able to make a bigger difference to society through a bigger organisation.'

THE TSWELELOPELE STRATEGY

In September 2017, Bothwell took up the CFO position at Kumba Iron Ore, which is part of the Anglo American group. His appointment was part of a shake-up in the company's leadership, which included Themba Mkhwanazi's appointment to the role of CEO a year before.

Kumba had gone through a tumultuous period prior to the changes and had experienced a massive downturn in financial performance due to a drop in global iron ore prices. Basic earnings per share declined from R33.44 in 2014 to R1.46 in 2015. This forced the company to reduce its mining footprint at its flagship Sishen mine and embark on a major retrenchment process.

'When I joined the company, the key thing was to ensure we were sufficiently competitive from a margin perspective to withstand the commodity price cycles,' Bothwell explains. 'In 2017 Themba conceived a great strategy called "Tswelelopele – Ore to Awe", which I helped implement. The strategy has three main premises: extracting full potential from our assets by making them more competitive; extending the life of our mines; and expanding our footprint.'

Tswelelopele is Setswana for 'moving forward', and Kumba has indeed been advancing since its implementation. One of the major targets was to save R2.6 billion in five years; the company achieved this goal in two and a half. The quality of their iron ore product has also improved, resulting in better pricing compared with that of their competitors. On top of that, the lifespan of the Sishen mine has been extended from 13 to 19 years and a project to convert the plant to enhance the quality of their iron ore products has been approved by the board.

'The highlight for me is that we have delivered value to our stakeholders through improved productivity and margin. Since 2018, our EBITDA [earnings before interest, taxes, depreciation and amortisation] margins have gone up from 45% to 70%, and with the increased profitability we've created R127 billion of shared value in taxation, royalties and dividends.

'Over and above payments to our employees, shareholders and the government, what I find particularly heart-warming is the support we've given to local businesses: since 2018 we've sourced R9 billion worth of goods and services from host-community suppliers, which helps to secure the livelihoods of communities around the mines. I consider it a great success story that we have moved from spending R500 million with host-community suppliers each year to a large multiple of that amount.'

Bothwell states that the key to success for any strategy starts with understanding the business, its purpose and its operational context in terms of the environment it operates in. Companies should focus on building resilience to ensure that they are profitable and sustainable, which, in turn, allows them to contribute to the preservation of livelihoods.

'Sustainability is a long-term concept, which can be achieved by understanding why you do what you do. For us, it was important to avoid having to go through another massive retrenchment process in the future. Having established our strategic direction, it made it easy to take the next step – setting up the building blocks. This included finding our competitive advantage, which is centred around ensuring we have quality product and extracting it safely and efficiently.'

Given the inherent risks in mining, it is sensible to follow a risk-based approach to setting out your strategy, Bothwell explains. This means performing a careful analysis for potential risks throughout the value chain and determining the elements necessary to manage them.

'Then it's all about a relentless push to meet the targets you have set for yourself. When there are setbacks, you need to understand the reasons for them and find ways to compensate. Strategy is also not a static thing; you need to scan your environment continually and evolve your strategy based on what is happening in that environment.'

An example of how strategy can evolve relates to how Kumba has approached the diversification of its customer base. For several years, the company relied heavily on sales to China, but there was a desire to have a more balanced share of other markets. Prior to the COVID-19 pandemic, they had reduced the proportion of sales to China from 80% to 55%. However, as China was one of the first countries to reopen its economy after global lockdowns, Kumba adjusted its strategy to increase sales in China, which helped protect the business in a challenging macro-environment. 'You need to be nimble as things change,' Bothwell advises.

The coronavirus pandemic brought about a prodigious dilemma for Kumba's management. The company makes such a mammoth contribution to the Northern Cape economy that if they were to stall operations, the province would be brought to its knees. The mine employs thousands of people from local communities and provides a number of district municipalities with water and medical services.

Bothwell says that while the company was unsure how many *lives* would be saved by shutting down the mine, they were certain how many *livelihoods* would be threatened if they did. And as protecting livelihoods is the central theme in their purpose, they took the decision to apply to the Minister of Mineral Resources and Energy to permit them to continue with reduced operations under strict health and safety protocols.

In addition, Kumba launched the WeCare programme, which undertook community education on preventative measures to halt the spread of the disease. They also provided material support in the form of food parcels, masks and sanitisers. Working with the Department of Health and local government, Kumba also provided critical medical supplies such as diagnostic equipment, ventilators, oxygen and quarantine facilities. At the time of our conversation, the company's vaccination drive was already underway and was set to extend to workers' families once the workforce was vaccinated. 'I believe we have done right by our people since the start of the pandemic and this is a personal highlight for me,' Bothwell beams.

PURPOSE-DRIVEN LEADERSHIP

As Head of Investor Relations at Kumba, Penny Himlok has to present the company to shareholders and analysts to ensure full and fair market valuation and transparent market feedback. In supporting the board of directors, she works closely with Bothwell.

'Bothwell is the kind of director who gives you a lot of space to grow,' says Penny. 'One thing he does is always to ask us what we think the company should do. That can be frustrating sometimes, because it would be easier if he just told us what to do! But I think it's his way of getting us to think like owners, to find our own purpose and also to develop our decision-making capability.'

'He's very strategic,' she continues. 'He has that ability to bring everything together; he surprises us with a fresh perspective to problem-solving by coming up with ideas that nobody else has thought of. I find him quite inspiring.'

Inspiring your team comes from focusing on both corporate and individual purpose. In one of the first strategy sessions Bothwell had with his finance team at Kumba, they spent a whole morning discussing purpose and why they do the things that they do.

'It took them by surprise, because as accountants we want to get down to the nitty-gritty and talk about things like cost management,' he recalls. 'But for me it's an important conversation, because once we are aligned in our reason for being, we can move on to discuss what that means in terms of the work we need to do to achieve our goals.'

Bothwell also tries to engage with the team to understand what is going on in their lives beyond work. He seeks to co-create rather than dictate because he believes in giving them the opportunity 'to do what we pay them to do, which is to bring their thoughts to the table. I also try to keep things light-hearted and laid-back. I trust my team to do what they are expected to do and I rarely get upset.

'Perhaps it's because I enjoy what I do and truly believe that I'm living out my purpose. I would advise young people to try and determine what they are passionate about early on and use that to drive their careers. That's a lot more powerful than blindly pursuing a high-paying job and driving a nice car.'

Bothwell also advises young professionals to remain consistent and be patient.

'When I was young, I was extremely impatient, particularly about the pace of getting promoted. When I was looked over for an opportunity, I was not willing to wait six months to progress to the next level. At the time, six months felt like an eternity, but in hindsight, it really wasn't! You can end up making the wrong decision simply because you're not patient enough for what is actually the right thing for you.'

Bothwell passes on such lessons to mentees as part of the group's global reciprocal mentorship programme, which is a two-way initiative with colleagues from across the Anglo American workforce. He is currently working with two individuals, one from Brazil and the other from Chile. 'It is quite enjoyable because we learn from each other,' he says.

Looking to the future, Bothwell sees himself participating actively in effecting change in his country of birth, Zimbabwe. 'This is despite my mother repeatedly discouraging me from going into politics,' he chuckles.

He is also passionate about combating gender-based violence, which is a prevalent vice in South Africa. As a father of twin daughters and a son, he would like to raise them in a better world and supports Kumba's movement to get men to acknowledge their role in creating a safe society and to become the driving voice behind eliminating this scourge.

Bothwell also sits on the board of the Cancer Association of South Africa, where he chairs the audit committee. He was involved with the audit of the organisation while at Deloitte and reached out to them after leaving the firm to volunteer his time. Having lost his father to cancer, he subscribes to the objective of the organisation to lead the fight against the disease.

Outside of work, Bothwell enjoys spending time with family, frequents the gym and occasionally plays tennis. As a long-suffering supporter of Liverpool, his collaborative leadership style is in keeping with the football club's mantra: 'You will never walk alone.'

BOIPELO LEKUBO

Born to shine

The offer of a full scholarship to study engineering at the University of the Witwatersrand was an attractive prospect indeed for matriculant Boipelo Lekubo, now Harmony Gold CFO. After all, she was good at both mathematics and science.

'It was definitely tempting,' she recalls. 'But I always wanted to be an accountant, so I declined the offer.'

In 2001, Boipelo enrolled at the University of Cape Town, the first step on her journey to becoming a chartered accountant. She graduated in 2003 and completed her honours degree at the University of Johannesburg the following year. As she had received a bursary from KPMG, she joined their offices in Pretoria after graduating.

'With the Pretoria office being smaller than the one in Johannesburg, I got to work in different sectors, pursuing a variety of tasks. It was a blessing in disguise, because many of my colleagues in bigger offices ended up specialising in a single sector. And often it is a sector that they did not chose in the first place.'

After completing her articles contract at KPMG, Boipelo was itching to leave auditing and get into the corporate arena. She accepted an offer to join Total Coal SA in January 2009. 'I enjoyed the interview and got the sense that it would be a great place to work. It ended up being a good decision, because I worked with Etienne Ferreira, who was a really wonderful mentor. I learnt a lot from him, including how to engage with third parties, working in teams and more about the technical aspects of my role.'

As group financial accountant, she had month-end reporting responsibilities and was supported by a team of accountants. 'We reported to the head office in Paris and the French really impressed me with how well they worked. They are very efficient; things are done properly during the month. Come month-end, it's only a matter of tying up loose ends and closing out the reporting. They have very good systems, which other companies should emulate.'

In search of career growth in the listed environment, Boipelo decided to join Northam Platinum in May 2012. It was a step up, as she was now responsible for budgeting and was involved in integrated reporting.

'It was a baptism of fire because I joined during year-end reporting and the pressure was on. The challenge became even harder because the head of finance fell ill. I had to assume the role and quickly learn to swim in the deep end. I'm glad to say that I managed to meet my targets and I learnt a lot in the process.'

TIME AT ATLATSA

In August 2014, Boipelo was head-hunted for the CFO role at Atlatsa Resources Corporation. She considered it a good move, because the company was listed on the Johannesburg, Toronto and New York stock exchanges, but admits it was rather intimidating going into the new position. She faced several challenges, including growing concerns about the operation struggling to generate sufficient cash flow.

'I was responsible for the financial well-being of the entity. We frequently had to interact with our colleagues in America on complex issues, including compliance with the requirements of the Securities and Exchange Commission. Our legal counsel were based in both New York and Canada, so the time differences were an additional thing to consider, given that virtual meeting platforms were not in common use at the time. We had to handle matters with people that we never saw and our discussions took place during abnormal working hours, which was a new experience for me.'

Harmony Gold's Boipelo Lekubo *(Photo: Harmony Gold)*

The operation was a joint venture with Anglo American Platinum, which Boipelo describes as a kind of big brother they constantly had to approach with a begging bowl when they needed additional funding. 'I experienced tremendous growth at Atlatsa. Soon after I left, the company was placed under care and maintenance, so I think it was admirable that we were able to stem that eventuality during my time there.'

During Boipelo's time at Atlatsa, they had to shut down two operations and retrench over 2 000 people in order to downsize and focus on core mining. 'At the time, platinum prices were depressed and production at the mine was not optimal,' Boipelo explains. Needless to say, the process of terminating jobs was not an easy task. 'It's easy to look at a spreadsheet and say, "Cut! Cut! Cut!" But for every cut, there's a person with a family to support and therefore livelihoods are impacted by the decision. The human element is profound, considering that the mining operation was also pivotal in the community.'

Whereas the labour relations department of Atlatsa dealt with the workers unions, Boipelo was involved in explaining the numbers. 'I remember this one time a trio of us – myself, the head of investor relations and the company secretary – were dispatched to meet the union leaders at the mine in Limpopo. I cannot forget the leaders' faces when three ladies walked into the room. Given local cultural perceptions, sending "a bunch of women" signified to them that management was not taking their concerns seriously. But we weathered the storm; we answered each of their questions adeptly and they eventually accepted the fact that there was no other option than to restructure the mine.'

Boipelo believes that effective communication is key for any financial leader hoping to achieve positive outcomes. 'The experience taught me that you need to communicate financial information in lay terms. But you also need to strike a balance and understand that employees comprehend many things. You should not treat them like children in explaining simple concepts such as sales, expenses, profits and losses.'

THE HARMONY EXPERIENCE

Boipelo joined Harmony as CFO in June 2017, again being head-hunted for the position. The prospect of working under financial director

Frank Abbott was attractive. 'What won me over was the opportunity to be mentored by Abbott, who is a seasoned financial leader in the gold mining industry.'

Boipelo's previous three stations averaged approximately 5 000 employees; at Harmony there are over 40 000. With ten different operations, Harmony is also a significantly bigger player than Atlatsa with its two sites and the single-operation Northam. Add to that a multi-jurisdictional aspect due to an operation in Papua New Guinea and it's clear that this job is not for the faint-hearted.

Her three years at Harmony so far have been eventful, from being involved in the accounting for major acquisitions to the integration of IT systems and team mergers. 'In 2018, we concluded a US$300 million acquisition of the Moab Khotsong mine from AngloGold Ashanti. And we've just [2020] acquired the last of AngloGold's South African assets, Mponeng and Mine Waste Solutions, for US$200 million cash, plus contingent consideration. The recapitalising of our Papua New Guinea mine was another very engaging activity, in addition to raising capital and refinancing debt. There's been a lot going on, but I must say I've also had fun in the process.'

In January 2020, Harmony announced that Abbott would be taking up the position of executive director responsible for business development. Boipelo's appointment to replace him as group financial director came just as the COVID-19 pandemic hit and the national state of disaster was declared in South Africa. 'The pandemic has brought challenges for my role and for our business. For instance, the capital raise we undertook in April [2020] was negotiated during lockdown, and we had to rely on virtual meetings to interact with the various parties.

She also explains that a mine cannot simply be 'switched off', as re-starting it would be very costly. 'Essential staff had to continue working during lockdown and fortunately, with the support of the Department of Mineral Resources, we were able to continue operating at 50% for the period immediately after the lockdown.'

An additional blessing for Harmony was that the gold price increased in this time, as the commodity is seen as a safe investment during times of uncertainty. This enabled the group to break even during the lockdown period.

Mining companies are price takers. So, an ill-considered ten-character tweet from an influential politician in the middle of the night can have a significant impact on the price of the product, and therefore revenue – a challenge that lies at the CFO's door.

'The CFO's work largely focuses on managing expenses. We take other measures to protect our margins, such as hedging. An additional issue we face is safety, because we operate deep underground, where seismic activity is a key issue. Safety is also a human behaviour matter; we have to worry about the steps 40 000 people are taking to protect themselves and others.'

As one of the youngest black female financial directors of a company on the Johannesburg Stock Exchange (JSE), Boipelo has seen her share of prejudice. 'There is frequently an unconscious bias in the workplace. Even if people don't say it out loud, you can sense it,' she says.

'But I think given my track record, it's clear that I'm not a token appointment. My experience speaks for itself, and in my dealings with people they quickly realise that I know what I'm talking about. I hasten to add that at Harmony transformation is a board agenda, so it is driven from the very top. Knowing that I'm supported by the highest organ of the group has made it easier for me to settle into my role.'

Being the financial director of a big JSE-listed company while being a mother of a pre-teen daughter is a challenge of a different kind. But, says Boipelo, she is thankful for having a lot of domestic support, which is helpful during busy periods and when she has to travel.

'We make the most of the time that we are together, and she is now at an age where she understands that mommy may not be able to pick her up from school every day.'

Asked how she would describe her management style, Boipelo calls it 'situational and inclusive'. 'I don't believe you can lead or manage with a blanket approach, because people are different,' she says.

'You must be able to read people. On one day you sense an employee is emotionally down and so you assign an outstanding task to someone else who can cope with it that day. In addition, you need to bring your people with you; they need to understand what the end goal is. If they understand where you're going, managing them becomes much easier.'

In November 2020, Boipelo was listed as one of the 100 Global

Inspirational Women in Mining by the non-profit organisation Women in Mining UK. Receiving the award was a humbling experience, she says, but also one of the proudest moments in her career so far.

ANDRÉ DU PLESSIS

The boy who sold his father's car

— INTERVIEW: OCTOBER 2020 —

'I'm more of an entrepreneur than an accountant,' reckons André du Plessis, CFO of Capitec, 'the world's best bank' according to its marketers. Indeed, as a fresh-faced Grade 1 boy somewhere in the 1960s, André sold his father's car!

'I was playing outside and for some reason, I ended up studying the vehicle and soon decided that it was time we exchanged it for something newer. So I set off looking for a buyer. I started talking to people to find out what would be a good price for the car and in the process got someone who was ready to talk to my father about buying it. My dad wasn't happy about it, but my mom thought it was a great idea, so eventually the car was sold.'

Besides an interest in business studies, André was fascinated with trees in his youth and harboured ambitions of studying forestry. But when he encountered the idea of chartered accountancy in the ninth grade, his career path was sealed.

'I studied accounting, but I've definitely never been your typical accountant. Even during my articles, I was more interested in understanding the businesses we were auditing. I wanted to learn what these companies did well, how they managed their finances and how they handled their clients. While my colleagues would simply execute a

Capitec's André du Plessis *(Photo: Lizelle Lotter)*

debtors circularisation as a matter of routine to verify debtors balances, I would identify such matters as overpricing and poor client relations from that area of audit.'

André pursued his articles contract in the mid-1980s with Arthur Andersen, one of the global Big Five audit firms at the time. He was transferred to the London office to pursue financial consulting and investment banking.

'I attribute a lot of my success to being in the right place at the right time, as well as making the best out of difficult situations. For instance, I studied accounting in Afrikaans and I therefore had a linguistic disadvantage when I joined an English-speaking firm. But I worked hard to excel in that unfamiliar environment. Similarly, when I arrived in the United Kingdom as a rank outsider, I always went the extra mile and made a success of it.'

As part of his first assignment during his stint in the London office, André was involved in a negotiation for the purchase of a Belgian business. Back then he was a mere 'suitcase carrier', a subordinate to be seen and not heard. Reluctant to accept his place, he angled for a deeper involvement in the transaction by asking to be at the negotiating table.

'Comforted by the fact that those across the table were from England, the Belgian group would speak to each other in Flemish during the negotiations. It is a Dutch dialect that's very similar to Afrikaans, so I could understand what they were saying. With that insight, I could relay critical information to our team that allowed a very successful outcome for us.'

André returned to South Africa to take up a management role in a new financial consulting business within Arthur Andersen South Africa. The division focused on financial markets undertaking activities such as mergers and acquisitions, business systems re-engineering and tax structuring.

JOURNEY INTO BANKING

André's father was a banker, as was his grandfather. So it came as no surprise when André followed in their footsteps in 1996 by leaving

Arthur Andersen to join Boland Bank. Incidentally, today one of his sons is also a banker.

'The bank's head office was based in the Western Cape and had been taken over by billionaire entrepreneur Christo Wiese. I joined the institution as Head of Finance, part of the team put together to turn the entity around. I really enjoyed the challenge of improving a problematic situation. A radical change was needed in the tax and capitalisation structure to keep the doors open.'

The team started looking at what the bank was doing, at the financial health of the businesses they served and where they could see market opportunities. They focused on taking complexities out so that the end user could benefit, André recalls. This brought many changes, including in terms of branding and personnel. 'I believe you should surround yourself with competence,' he says firmly.

In August 1998, Boland Bank merged with NBS (the Natal Building Society) and BoE (the Board of Executors) Bank and André was appointed as CFO of the merged entity. With the bank being based in Durban, he had to commute between his home in Cape Town and the office every week, something he found torturous.

'It was not just the commute that made that stint horrible for me; working at the merged entity was unbearable. Everybody looked at bonus rules before making decisions. Consequently, we struggled to formulate a concrete strategy. Manager A may have needed to make a success of Project 1 to maximise his remuneration while Manager B wanted Project 2 to fly for the same reason. As a result, the two were unable to work together.'

After a year, André and some of his colleagues resigned and took a four-month sabbatical, during which they crafted the concept that gave birth to the Capitec dream. The founders included Michiel le Roux, Riaan Stassen, Christian van Schalkwyk, Carl Fisher, Chris Oosthuizen and André Olivier.

'Others who joined us were Gerrie Fourie, who was working in the liquor industry at the time, and Leon Venter, from the telecoms industry. Jannie Mouton and Chris Otto from PSG provided 90% of the initial capital. We bought a shell known as The Business Bank and started off with a handsome tax loss.'

Capitec Bank listed on the Johannesburg Stock Exchange (JSE) in February 2002. From its early years, it set out to be a low-cost mass-market retail bank, with the objective of establishing paperless banking – with no customer ever having to fill out a form. From a few hundred employees, the bank has grown to a workforce of over 14 000 and 15 million active clients today.

HIGHS AND LOWS AT CAPITEC

'Capitec has been the single most significant achievement of my life,' André says. 'It has turned out to be the most successful entity PSG has invested in and it is testament to the adage that hard work pays. We've won several accolades over the years, including being recognised as the best bank in the world by the Lafferty Group's Global Bank Quality benchmarking study. Brand Finance recognised the company as the third strongest banking brand in the world in early 2020.'

Capitec's brand promise is centred around four basic principles: simplicity, affordability, accessibility, and personal service.

'We measure ourselves against innovation and total transparency. If a product does not meet these criteria, we do not take it to the market. Banking is quite simple, although many people don't understand it. The reason for our focus on simplicity is that it's the easiest way to achieve financial inclusion, which is quite important in South Africa. During apartheid, banks only looked after a tenth of the population. It's been a big achievement for us to make banking less of a grudge purchase; it's now a product that is accessible and affordable to everyone.'

The industry recognises André's contributions, and he received both the Compliance & Governance award and the Finance & Technology award from CFO South Africa in 2019. He also scooped the 2019 CFO of the Year award at CNBC Africa's All Africa Business Leaders Awards.

'I credit my team with these recognitions. We cannot do it without the people who work for us. These accolades belong to a team, not to an individual. I have a huge issue with people in management who see things from the "I" rather than the "we" perspective. When things go well, people want to be recognised as individuals, yet when things go wrong, they want to look around and bring others in to share the blame instead of using that as an opportunity to consider what they, as individuals, could have done better.'

André considers both the jobs they have created and the opportunity to help the previously unbanked as highlights of his career.

'We're training and equipping people … helping them to grow. We're helping our customers and staff build a credit record that will enable them to build homes and take loans for worthwhile causes such as education. Our fees are very affordable; the mere fact that we entered the market saves South Africans R20 billion in bank charges annually.'

However, the journey has not had only highlights. One of the lows of André's career came on 30 January 2018.

'On 29 January we went to bed as heroes, but shortly after we woke up on the 30th we were zeroes. It is a lesson in remaining humble at all times.'

On that fateful morning, Capitec management woke up to the news that Viceroy Research had published a document accusing the bank of massive overstatement of financial assets and reckless lending practices. They claimed that the bank was 'simply uninvestable'.

'To be accused of dishonesty was extremely upsetting. We had to accept that success breeds scrutiny. You cannot control what others say about you; how you react to it is what matters. We were very swift with our reaction and issued two SENS [Stock Exchange News Service] announcements that same day and rapidly convened a Bloomberg news conference. We also had over 700 lines open where investors could dial in for us to address any concerns.'

André believes the entire 'exposé' was fabricated by the Delaware-based research company to short sell Capitec stock. Viceroy Research's website disclaimer indeed makes it clear that the authors may have direct or indirect interests in all stocks and could well benefit from any price declines.

'What I learnt from the Viceroy experience was how to deal with a crisis. If you told me two years ago that because of a global pandemic we would have to send over 3 000 call centre agents home to work from there, I might have said we would not survive. But we've learnt that you have two choices when the unexpected happens: you can choose to be a victim, or you can choose to take it on the chin and make a plan. It is for that reason that the bank has performed well, despite the COVID-19 pandemic.'

People generally do not phone André with good news. But for him that is a good thing. 'If people call you when things are not going well, it shows that you're dependable. You should be concerned if you are not called upon in moments of crisis.

'A banker never sleeps well, because we are dealing with issues of money, technology, credit risk … Managing an operation that processes 6000 transactions per second means that if something goes wrong, it can be catastrophic. This calls for a mindset of thinking straight and acting straight. My approach is to consult colleagues, have robust stakeholder discussions, engage in fervent prayer and gather critical information to make the best decision.'

LIFE BEYOND BANKING

André is a devout Christian who strives also to have an impact on the community by helping the less fortunate. His family – wife, Elsabe, and sons, Jean-Pierre, Jacques and Francois – support an orphaned child in the Eastern Cape, which made them aware of the emotional challenges facing children in poor communities.

As a result, he partnered with a social worker, Philip Geldenhuys, to launch Community Keepers, a non-profit organisation that provides counselling services to over 2 700 underprivileged children in the Western Cape annually.

'Our family and friends raised the funds to start the organisation, and since then it has depended on support from individuals and corporates. The real heroes are the thirty-one social workers, ten counsellors, six psychologists and other staff who support these children on a daily basis. The testimonials we've received are really heart-warming; we're making a difference in these young lives.'

André is also passionate about mentorship. Many people approach him for guidance, and as he approaches eventual retirement, he is grooming the next lot of finance leaders in Capitec to 'run the company for the next hundred years'.

'In the short term our plans are to get the company back on track after the COVID-19 crisis. We have new products and services in the pipeline. We recently purchased Mercantile Bank, which we intend to position as an institution that serves small and medium-sized entities.'

André, who loves the outdoors and has climbed Mount Kilimanjaro and travelled through 58 countries on his motorbike, plans to retire in 2022. He looks forward to having more time to travel the world with his wife, 'take care of my dogs and hopefully welcome some grandkids', he says with a laugh.

Retirement might be an opportunity to take his outdoor exploits to new levels. But who knows what else this entrepreneur–accountant might get up to?

AARTI TAKOORDEEN

How a poor child from Ladysmith became
SA's youngest listed-company CFO

— INTERVIEW: AUGUST 2021 —

There are probably very few, if any, chief financial officers of South Africa's top companies who have ever had to go to bed hungry. Aarti Takoordeen may be the CFO of the Johannesburg Stock Exchange (JSE) today, but she still has vivid memories of the hunger she experienced growing up in Ladysmith in a family of four with a single parent.

At 32, Aarti was the youngest appointed CFO of a main board JSE listed entity in 2013: the JSE itself. The JSE is a securities exchange that provides a primary market, secondary market and post-trade services, market data and technology services and also regulates markets.

Aarti's mother worked as a receptionist at Chisa Welding in Ladysmith and struggled to make ends meet on her modest salary. Although she and her siblings grew up in a loving home, there were days when there wasn't enough to eat, and Aarti knew her mother would never be able to afford to send her to university.

She was a good student and matriculated at the age of 17 from Windsor Secondary School in Ladysmith in 1997. But she was unsure about what career to pursue. Her mother prodded her to consider joining 'a team of people in suits' she saw showing up once a year at Chisa, speaking flowery English and commanding the respect of all the workers on the premises. The description was sufficient to persuade Aarti to

The JSE's Aarti Takoordeen *(Photo: Patrick Furter)*

apply for an article contract at Reyneke & Erasmus, a local auditing out-fit in town. Impressed with her matric results, they were convinced that she would be able to pursue a degree and complete a training contract at the same time.

Motivated to lift herself and her family out of poverty, Aarti enrolled for accounting studies at the University of South Africa in 1998. She graduated with a Bachelor of Accounting Science degree in 2002 and completed her honours in the same discipline a year later. In 2004, she wrote her board examinations and qualified as a chartered accountant.

Aarti joined Hewlett Packard's Johannesburg office in October 2004 as head of commercial finance, where she 'put her hand up for everything over and above her day job'. Apart from overseeing day-to-day account-ing and finances, her role also involved drawing insights from financial data to put focused, operationally supported strategies in place to ensure the company's return on investment through mergers and acquisitions.

Being exposed to the commercial aspects of an IT services group was very fulfilling, and just the right training ground for her next role: group financial director of Johnson Controls for the Middle East and Africa, which she took up in 2009.

The job at Johnson Controls was challenging and demanding but she had little input in the strategic direction of the company, as this was determined at the international head office. Aarti was in line to become managing director. But the prestigious title did not excite her: she had a nagging desire to be somewhere where she could contribute to shaping a company.

After a while, she began considering other local opportunities. So, when Nicky Newton-King, then CEO of the JSE, approached her in 2013, she did not think twice about accepting the offer to be CFO at the institution. A year later she was recognised by CFO South Africa as Young CFO of the Year.

In 2017, she was selected to join the World Economic Forum's five-year programme for Young Global Leaders, which is aimed at bringing together individuals under the age of 40 to tackle some of the world's most complex challenges through innovative solutions. Her participa-tion in this programme and the transformation she has been part of at the JSE count among Aarti's career highlights. When she joined the

JSE, the leadership of the Exchange was predominantly white and male. Today, three-quarters of the top management comprises women and the rest of the organisation is also much more diverse.

STRATEGY AND LEADERSHIP

Aarti regards strong values and a true focus on people as key drivers for business decisions, which made the three-month executive education programme she completed through the Harvard Business School in 2021 all the more fulfilling.

'The programme had to be run online because of the [COVID-19] pandemic. But this turned out to be an advantage, because some of the speakers who would ordinarily not have made it to the Harvard campus managed to speak to us virtually.' What stood out for Aarti was that every speaker emphasised focusing on people as an integral part of business strategy. 'To be successful, everything we do needs to be people centred and people driven,' she explains.

'Strategy is set through your purpose as an organisation. If your purpose is centred around uplifting the society where you operate, I think profits will follow naturally. It is also important that your strategy is informed by positive guiding principles such as transparency, ethics and integrity.'

Strategies fail when the values meant to facilitate their execution are paid lip service. This, Aarti says, is usually due to poor leadership, with the positive principles penned in strategy documents remaining nothing but words.

'Another problem is a lack of responsiveness, and this has a lot to do with paying attention to your operating environment. Over the years, not many large organisations have shown this responsiveness to society, but I think we're seeing a genuine effort to transform companies into a force for good, as employers and leaders start to recognise the benefits of social involvement.'

Strategies also fail when leaders struggle to shift gears when needed. 'Ambidexterity is essential – being strong in delivering on the hardcore objectives while, at the same time, having a view of where the rest of the pack is headed,' says Aarti. 'At the JSE, we don't rate managers highly if they shoot the lights out but leave their team members behind.'

She has learnt how important it is for an organisation's leadership to focus on employees' professional growth, which is underpinned by their empowerment. This entails exposing individuals to diverse situations and giving them the autonomy to work without being micromanaged.

'I don't run my team in a hierarchical way. We build deep relationships and connections in the team, all the way down to the most junior person. My approach is development friendly. I'm not an unrelatable or untouchable leader; I take a keen interest in the individual stories of every team member.'

Aarti takes the time to connect personally with everyone in her 25-member finance team at least twice a year. She has weekly meetings with her direct reports and meets with the whole team at least once a month.

Her focus on building real relationships has helped her and the team through the challenging times brought on by the COVID-19 pandemic, which has claimed two of her team members. 'I appreciate the importance of a human connection and so does the entire company leadership. The JSE availed counselling and brought in a guest speaker to talk to the team about grief in a town hall session.'

Having had to deal with the passing of her husband in 2020, Aarti is keenly aware of the impact of losing someone close to you. She believes it is important to acknowledge the power of the healing process. If people are not allowed enough time to work through their grief, it can easily lead to post-traumatic stress.

She regularly checked in with team members she noticed taking strain after the passing of their colleague, either through a text message or a telephone call. Often, she would reach out to them on a Sunday, when their conversation would not be bound by the rigours of the working week. And her personal assistant remains under instruction to prioritise any requests from her team for one-on-one catch-up appointments.

ADVICE

Looking back, Aarti wishes she had extended her people focus beyond work. Today she knows it is important to develop deep connections with people both at work and in your private life. 'The full circle of life means that the people you encounter are likely to come back into your life at some point later. How you treat them today has a direct effect on your future.'

Aarti encourages young professionals to strive to always be the best version of themselves. For that, she says, you should establish what your value system is at the start of your career, and let it guide you throughout. Young professionals should hold themselves to account through both their words and their actions.

When it comes to recruiting and promoting employees, attitude weighs more than academic excellence for Aarti. 'You can teach people technical information, but you cannot really teach a constructive attitude.'

She also admires individuals who exhibit resilience and courage. But ambition should be combined with a good dose of empathy. It doesn't help if you can get the job done but lack in the softer metrics, she says.

As a young Indian woman, Aarti has experienced bias around her age, her religion, her race and her gender. But she does not waste too much time or energy on such incidents. 'I play my own game and put my head down to deliver. The solution for discrimination is to prove your competence.'

That said, she did tackle the transformation battle at the JSE head on because of its wider impact in the organisation. 'Early on when I joined the institution, there were certain inflection points when, as leaders, we had to stop a meeting to question whether we're treating people equally. It is important, in my view, to have the courage to call out bias. It's an energy-sapping exercise because these conversations are difficult, and can drive you to tears. But you need to have them because that's the only way you will effect change.' The road to transformation has been an emotional journey for Aarti because she believes we should, as a country, have made greater progress in this regard than we have.

Being in charge of the company's finances can be stressful and Aarti is thankful that the JSE is a fitness-focused organisation. She runs and does yoga with people from work and meditation sessions are scheduled in everyone's diaries. 'It is important to find ways to relieve pressure. No two days are the same here; one day the systems could be down and on another something like a downgrade announcement can cause an upset.'

When it comes to managing a crisis, Aarti has solid advice: don't panic! Panic only leads to ill-considered decisions. Stay calm, she says, and take a step back to think about different options and possible consequences of each.

'I read about a CEO who sent a note to the organisation when a crisis hit,' Aarti recounts. 'It was a well-written memo drafted spontaneously, but the CEO did not consider that the email could be forwarded to people outside the organisation and have far-reaching consequences for the company. It resulted in a colossal tumble of the company's share price, which they're yet to recover from. I think it is important to always test your thinking with others around the table and so uncover ideas that you may not have thought about.'

In a crisis it is so easy to give in to the flight-or-fight response, she cautions, because you want to fix the problem as quickly as possible. Rather than running, stand still for a moment, she says. Think before you act. This has been a difficult lesson to learn – even for her, because by her own admission, she has the kind of personality that wants to get control back as quickly as possible when a crisis strikes.

In her private time, Aarti loves to read, whether fiction or non-fiction. For leadership and management lessons, she recommends *The Ride of a Lifetime* by Robert Iger, who ran the Walt Disney Company for 15 years.

'*Becoming* by Michelle Obama is another book I really enjoyed. It is a bit slow, but she has a nice, gentle and political way of getting her point across. I could relate a lot to her story, including how she grew up, how she started in the workplace and how she was judged. Like her, I experienced impostor syndrome, as well as the pressure of wanting – and needing – to be better in the eyes of your community.'

At 40, the once poor girl from Ladysmith has already achieved so much. One suspects that Aarti Takoordeen's remarkable journey, like Michelle Obama's, will continue to bring growth and great achievements.

GRATHEL MOTAU

Paradigm of trust

— INTERVIEW: AUGUST 2021 —

'Perhaps I could try to do what your boss does,' an 18-year-old Grathel Motau told her mom, a domestic worker, one day in January 1993. 'I would love to drive a BMW as nice as hers!'

That day Grathel was discussing her career options at the home in Douglasdale where her mother worked. Her mom's employer was Beverley Cooke, the first female partner at KPMG South Africa. The conversation led to a meeting with Beverley, who not only explained to Grathel what she did but offered to pay for her accounting studies at the University of South Africa.

Grathel graduated with a BCompt Accounting degree in 1995. She was the first one in her family to get a degree, inspired by her teachers' encouragement that she could do anything as long as she worked hard. This belief and the profound desire to lift her family out of poverty urged her to complete her degree despite her dislike for mathematics and numbers.

In 1997, she joined KPMG as an article clerk, working in the Services and Trading division. She successfully completed an honours degree in accounting, studying part time, and qualified as a chartered accountant in March 2000.

'I left KPMG three months after qualifying and quickly learnt an important life lesson,' Grathel reveals. 'It is often a wrong decision to base a professional move on the amount of money a company offers you. I chose Vodacom over the IDC [Industrial Development Corporation] because the pay was better by R20 000 a year. A week into my job, I realised I'd made a mistake, because the tasks I was assigned were very monotonous. I went back to the IDC to ask if they would still have me.'

Grathel spoke to Andile Reve, who was the vice-president of the IDC at the time. Reve told her that you don't simply walk away from a mistake and its consequences. He would be happy to have her at the IDC, he said, but only after she had completed three months' probation at Vodacom.

Grathel subsequently joined the IDC as a deal maker in June 2000, where her role included performing due diligences, deal origination and structuring equity and loan transactions in the electrical, electronics, telecommunications and IT sectors.

TIME AT NATIONAL TREASURY, AMABUBESI AND BLUE IQ

Nearly four years later, she was keen to broaden her horizons and accepted a position at the National Treasury as director of asset and liability management in the energy and communications sectors. Here she was responsible for restructuring entities such as Eskom, the South African Broadcasting Corporation, PetroSA and Telkom. All requests related to the Public Finance Management Act crossed her desk, after which she would put together a memo for approval by the then Minister of Finance, Trevor Manuel. Key transactions at the time included the large borrowing plan for the construction of the Medupi and Kusile power stations.

Leaving Treasury after only a year was one of the hardest career moves Grathel has ever had to make. She loved the job because the institutional culture was very professional, and of course she was directly exposed to the pulse of the South African economy. The work was challenging in a positive way; she had to draft thoroughly researched memos for the minister and also dealt with rating agencies, who relied on her department for critical information to rate government's performance.

The downside was that the job entailed working very long hours.

Thebe Investment Corporation's Grathel Motau *(Photo: Harmony Gold)*

59

She would drive back from the Pretoria office after working most of the night just in time to shower, change and drop her son at school before heading back to the office again. She resigned in April 2005 and left for Amabubesi Investments (now NMT Capital) despite pleas by Lesetja Kganyago, then the director general, to stay on. 'If, back then, we had been living in a virtual world like today, I would have stayed on and worked from home,' she observes.

Grathel was appointed head of the Amabubesi Investment Fund responsible for the disbursement of over R100 million to a selection of investments. The fund excelled on the back of a couple of sound deals. For example, they purchased a stake in Pinnacle Technologies at a time when a share was valued at 80c and exited when the price had risen to R4. Another choice investment was Lancewood Cheese, which has since become a household brand.

In May 2007, Grathel was approached to take up the role of group CFO of Blue IQ Investments, the brainchild of the Gauteng provincial government, aimed at partnering with the private sector to promote investment in growth industries. This was Grathel's first time in the role of finance director and it was a time of great learning on how to lead people, take accountability for an entire finance department and implement policies, systems and procedures.

It was also her first experience of seeing the potential impact of politics on business. Her stint at the organisation lasted just over two years, as interference from politicians led to changes in the leadership of the organisation that she did not agree with.

BACK AT KPMG AND TRANSITION TO THEBE

She returned to KPMG in October 2009 as an audit partner, with the understanding that she would transition to Advisory Services over time. 'When I returned to KPMG, I needed to understand the organisation all over again,' Grathel says. 'I'd been away for over nine years and it was now a different company with different people, a different culture and an evolved audit methodology. I was in the energy and resources department and responsible for the audit of Eskom. I signed off the last audit done by KPMG in 2014 before SNG Grant Thornton took over.'

In 2015, the KPMG leadership changed, which included the retirement of CEO Moses Kgosana and the election of Trevor Hoole in his place. The head of advisory services also left his post and Grathel did not feel the new executive committee would be supportive of her intended move to the division. She decided to take a year off, spend time with her family and complete her master's degree in development finance through Stellenbosch University.

During her sabbatical, Grathel became a media commentator and regular appeared on SAfm, Power FM and CNBC Africa to discuss matters related to finance and the South African economy. She really enjoyed this, as it was so completely different from what she had done up to that point, and she encourages fellow accountants to seek similar opportunities to be more than just 'bean counters'.

Grathel also trained to become an executive coach. 'I've always wanted to help empower people and found coaching to be very impactful and transformational. To date, I have been holding weekly coaching sessions with my team and use every single opportunity I can find as a coaching moment. This approach also aids my own development and helps me to have an open mind most of the time.'

With an entrepreneurial mindset, Grathel started her own firm, Mmoni Advisory Services, while at the same time serving on credit committees for FirstRand and the IDC, and also on various boards as a non-executive director. Then, in mid-2020, a recruiter called to ask if she could assist with CVs of potential candidates for the role of group CFO at the Thebe Investment Corporation. She provided her with the names and contacts of several people she thought would be suitable for the job. The recruiter called a couple of days later explaining that Thebe's management was actually more interested in Grathel herself than the people she had recommended.

'I told her I was not available, and she should not phone me again if she was looking to offer me the job,' Grathel states. 'I felt that I was too busy to take on a full-time role. Besides, I had just launched my executive coaching website and was hoping to finally maximise the skills I had acquired qualifying as an executive coach.'

Then on a lazy Sunday evening at a friend's house, the topic of the Thebe job came up again. As they slowly downed a bottle of champagne on the patio, Grathel recounted the conversation with the recruiter. Her host, Musa Mzoneli, coincidentally a friend of Thebe's CEO Sizwe Mncwango, urged Grathel not to be dismissive and insisted on introducing her to him the following day in a phone call. After the introduction, Sizwe convinced Grathel to consider engaging in the recruitment discussions with Thebe. After a 'challenging' recruitment process, she was appointed with effect from September 2020.

She's not looked back since. 'Thebe is an environment that's ready to embrace new ideas, new thinking and new people,' Grathel says. 'The company has people who have been there for years and who've helped me to understand the complexities and challenges of the organisation. I realised early on that to succeed, I need to recruit people who are cleverer than I am. Working with these people has really made me proud: I got to witness true black excellence.'

CAREER LESSONS

Grathel's advice to young professionals is to nurture relationships. She believes her career has progressed largely as a result of the bonds she has developed and maintained with people in all the companies she has worked for.

'I also recommend asking for help,' Grathel continues. 'People are always ready to offer counsel; you just need to ask. In addition, try and be curious all the time and have a mind that is open to learning new things. This includes things outside of finance. As I mentioned, one of the things I'm most proud of is sharing the stage on TV with top economists. Finally, be true to yourself.'

Asked about dealing with challenges, Grathel says you should see them for what they are. Often you interpret a situation differently from what it really is. Keep in mind that your truth is not always everyone else's truth, and try to understand things from someone else's perspective if you want a rounded view on matters. What you may have thought a crisis, might even turn out not to be. And if it really is one, there is always a solution.

She also points out that it doesn't help to panic. Instead, she says, seek guidance from competent people – put your heads together and find a way to overcome the problem. Furthermore, it is important to identify people who you can trust as mentors and can call upon when you're struggling with a problem. At a management level, having an executive coach can help you to get clarity about your goals, maximise your strengths and develop appropriate responses to situations.

From time to time, the work environment will present situations that are testing, and one needs to learn how to navigate conflict with clients and colleagues. Grathel recalls a time at KPMG when a senior partner who really supported her felt it necessary to take over a meeting with a cantankerous client.

'It was a humiliating experience because I felt like he did not believe I could handle the situation on my own,' Grathel recalls. 'I went to the bathroom and had a good cry. Then I asked the senior partner for a meeting to discuss what had happened. I made it clear that although I appreciated his support, he didn't need to act as a protector because I'm more than capable of standing on my own.'

Grathel was glad she had the discussion with her colleague, who had not realised his behaviour was disempowering her. The experience taught her that you should stand your ground and not shy away from having difficult conversations. Raising issues tactfully may be difficult, but in the long run it will earn you the respect of your co-workers.

A management lesson Grathel loves to share is the need to be understanding of other people. Empathy is very important, but at the same time a leader also needs to push people beyond what they believe they can do. She has found that many people, especially women, often do not believe that they are good enough. They often think of themselves in a negative way and need someone to nudge them to realise their potential.

According to Grathel a good manager leads by example, earning their trust and showing them what the possibilities for success are. She also believes you should not hesitate to admit that you do not always have the answers. 'Moreover, you need to show people that you are listening to them. What doesn't make sense to you may make sense to them, and by listening to their input, you might uncover a silver bullet that benefits the team.'

Grathel's teenage desire to drive a BMW may have led her into a career in accounting, but she has since shifted her automotive preference to Toyota. And speaking of cars, her favourite read is *The Monk who Sold his Ferrari* by Robin Sharma, because it reminds readers to think about the legacy they will leave behind. 'Material things – like the fancy cars we drive – don't matter. It is about our being and our experience of the world. We're here to make our experience appreciable for other people so that we may be remembered favourably when we are gone.'

Another book she recently read which she recommends for professionals is *The Speed of Trust: The One Thing that Changes Everything* by Stephen Covey. With a lack of trust little is achieved; its absence slows things down. Grathel gives the example of asking a team member to prepare a report, but receiving a document littered with errors. This means she cannot trust the team member to do their job properly and the next time she receives a report she will need to check it thoroughly, losing a lot of time.

'We should pursue all available avenues to develop trust, because the faster we do that, the quicker our businesses can reach their goals. Trust is the glue that builds collaboration and drives performance,' she concludes.

GLENN FULLERTON

The man who doctors said would never work again

— INTERVIEW: JULY 2021 —

After working for several listed entities, including Rembrandt and Malbak, which included Kohler Packaging and SA Druggists (later Aspen) in the 1990s, Glenn Fullerton was appointed CFO of the MB Technologies Group (MBT, today known as the Tarsus Technology Group) in 2000. This chartered accountant and cycling enthusiast subsequently became the CEO of Africa's largest technology distributor. In his spare time, Glenn took part in many endurance events, such as the 116-kilometre Ride for Sight race in Johannesburg in February 2013.

All was going well, and Glenn was confident he would complete the race in his fastest time. But then, with only 10 kilometres to go, on a steep downhill, two bikes ahead of him suddenly had a violent coming together. Glenn had no time to react. He went flying over his handlebars, crashing violently into the hot tarmac, with his head, neck, right shoulder and ribs breaking his fall.

As the paramedics attended to Glenn, tears streamed down his face. The searing pain he experienced told him he had sustained very serious injuries. His thoughts flashed to his former boss, Leo Baxter, founder of Tarsus Technologies and MBT, whose life was turned upside down in 2007 when he had a terrible accident while playing polo that left him with quadriplegia. After his accident, Leo continued to chair board meetings, during which Glenn would assist him with tasks such as turning the pages of reports, giving him something to drink and putting on his glasses.

Lying on the tarmac that day, he knew he'd been lucky to survive; the good news was that he didn't die. The bad news was that medical specialists later told him he would never be able to work again, and was likely to face permanent disability. He stubbornly refused to accept this.

Glenn had experienced what doctors call vertical shearing of a portion of the right side of his brain, which affected his short-term memory – to such an extent that he would typically forget a person's name two minutes after an introduction. He was housebound for months and went through multiple surgeries and extensive physiotherapy to help him regain mobility.

Before the accident, among his corporate roles, Glenn was the chairman of the company's provident fund, which offered extensive insurance covers including death and disability benefits. He never thought he would be a beneficiary of the fund and is thankful to this day for the support he had during the two years of rehabilitation. It was the lowest point of his life, a period of severe shoulder, neck and rib pain and headaches – even the smallest bump in the road when being driven to the hospital for treatment felt like someone was cutting his neck with a hacksaw.

Other than his physical struggles, his mental health was challenged by a sense of abandonment. 'What I learnt from the experience was that your health is the number one asset on your balance sheet,' Glenn says.

'Your next best assets are your family and close friends, who will be with you during times of adversity. The business world moves on quickly and corporates will replace you at the drop of a hat as they have investor returns to worry about. You quickly become lonely, because even if people mean well, they get busy and before they know it, a month has passed without them having checked on you. The days were long and the nights extremely painful during the time I recovered from my injuries.'

It took tremendous willpower and countless hours of therapy for Glenn to regain his short-term memory and physical well-being. His tenacious and optimistic personality was tested to the limit. With a

Nampak's Glenn Fullerton *(Photo: Sigil Photography)*

never-say-die attitude, he maintained a resolve to overcome this hurdle life had thrown his way – testament to the human spirit being able to overcome adversity with grit and the determination to succeed.

As a young man, Glenn's father, also a chartered accountant, inculcated in him a love of finance. Every Sunday, they would pull out the business section of the newspaper and pick out stocks, then check how their choices were doing the following week. It was his father who urged Glenn to capitalise on his leadership skills (he had been head prefect of Jeppe High School for Boys), to qualify as an accountant and not to think he could make a career out of his passion for cricket.

After high school, he joined Deloitte for articles while studying accounting part time through the University of South Africa and playing premier league cricket on weekends. He qualified as a chartered accountant in 1993.

Given the extent of his injuries, Glenn resigned from MBT to focus on his rehabilitation. He was determined to contribute and lead a team of people in the business world again. After his recovery, a professional contact recommended him as a candidate for the CFO position at Nampak, Africa's largest packaging group. He was appointed in September 2015.

STEERING A SHIP IN STORMY WEATHER

Upon joining Nampak, Glenn was faced with a company under the strain of high debt levels due to its investments in the rest of the African continent. On the back of the rising African narrative, the group had disposed of South African-based business with low margins and low barriers, and invested heavily to enter the market in Angola and Nigeria. Both countries are oil-dependent economies that rely on the sale of the volatile resource for their foreign exchange inflows. When the oil price nose-dived in 2015, the countries restricted dollar outflow and unpegged their respective exchange rates. This negatively impacted Nampak's Angolan and Nigerian operations.

In addition, the group had investments in Zimbabwe, where hyperinflation meant the local currency would depreciate from a one-to-one relationship with the US dollar to Z$88 to one greenback by

September 2021. Despite Nampak's best efforts, the macroeconomic factors in these countries have placed the group's profitability – and consequently its share price – under pressure.

'To add to our troubles, the COVID-19 pandemic hit Africa hard last year, and it's had a really negative impact on our business,' Glenn says. 'For us a beverage can manufacturer, a significant market segment is the entertainment industry, which has been under varying levels of lockdown since March 2020. We're grateful for having built very good relationships with our lenders, who have supported us during this tumultuous time.'

But even before COVID-19, Nampak's market positioning was impacted by stiff competition from two new entrants into the South African canning market. These factors have made Glenn's job much more difficult than that of CFOs heading companies in flourishing industries. But he is not complaining.

'When the tide rises in certain seas and lifts all the boats there, the captains have it easy. But in seas with pounding rain and choppy waves, a captain must navigate to keep the vessel afloat. When the storm is over, those captains who had to grind to survive will have honed their skills much more than those who coasted through tranquil waters.'

Glenn believes that although we all strive to win, having our skills tested in times of adversity means that a lot more can be learnt than sailing through easy times. One of his favourite quotes is from Martin Luther King: 'The ultimate measure of a man is not where he stands in moments of comfort and convenience, but where he stands at times of challenge and controversy.'

Yes, the last six years have been challenging, says Glenn, but he is confident that he has learnt a great deal to successfully steady the Nampak ship in these uncertain times.

Scenario planning is important, because to steer a ship you have to know whether to go right or left, and how much right and how much left. But he cautions against getting caught up in analysis paralysis. Simply get to a point where you understand the cause and effect of your decisions – the key is to make the best decisions possible after having applied the necessary due diligence.

Based on his experience at Nampak, Glenn says it is important to work closely with your funding partners and ensure that, in both good and bad times, there is clear communication and delivery against forecasts. For a group CFO, this means doing thorough review on internal forecasts, having intimate knowledge of the business and being equipped with an in-depth understanding of the impacts of key drivers in the respective group operations. This becomes extremely complex when dealing with operations across various geographies and with complex foreign exchange issues.

ADVICE

Young professionals should know that things do not always go as planned and graphs do not always rise in a straight line. Sometimes, despite the best efforts of management, external forces work against the company and those are moments that call for level heads. In addition, it is important to seek counsel from the more seasoned members of the team.

'The young community today lean heavily on Google as their source of information,' Glenn observes. 'It is indeed a tremendous source of information, but they should not discount lessons from real people, with scars on their backs. I'm grateful to have learnt so much from my late father, who gained deep insights into the business world in his role as manager of the Inspectorate Department of the JSE [Johannesburg Stock Exchange]. He would always emphasise the importance of integrity, since he investigated many people whose ethical lapses led to long jail terms.'

Glenn advises managers to take time to get to know each team member and their personal journeys. Management should also encourage open debate, idea sharing and building unity. Having respect for everybody's opinion is key in creating a sense of belonging among staff. He points out that professionals should avoid thinking that their credentials make them more important than the team; often the best answer to a question comes from the people you least expect.

It is important to manage both upwards and downwards, Glenn says. This means listening as much to the team below you as to the inputs from the board, and as such an executive team member has to build good relationships with non-executive directors. In the past, Glenn has witnessed friction between executive and non-executive board members, often because those in non-executive positions do not appreciate the practical difficulties of running a business.

Although the CFO's job can be draining, Glenn has developed a level of resilience over the years. His wife, Lauren, who is also a chartered accountant, understands his rigorous obligations. He works very long hours and usually sleeps only for six hours, which he concedes is insufficient. Pastimes that help him relieve stress include quality time with his family, weekend bicycle rides and two rounds of golf each month.

Whereas the cycling accident was undoubtedly the lowlight of Glenn's life, marrying Lauren and having three children are, without question, highlights. 'Watching Gareth, Cameron and Katherine come into this world and grow up to be wonderful human beings eclipses anything I've ever achieved professionally. They have performed impeccably in both sports and academics. But above all, they've grown up to be people of good character, with unquestionable integrity and a high work ethic. My family is extremely important to me.'

Glenn is a fan of Robin Sharma's books. He recently read *The 5AM Club*, which explores the idea of organising your thoughts in the morning and trying to direct your life to where you want it to go. The book also cautions against digital distractions, a view that Glenn supports as he believes 'email and social media are a modern-day pandemic characterised by a barrage of information that results in a wasted energy.'

He says his 'middle-aged frame may creak and experience pain from time to time', but Glenn lives a life of gratitude, knowing that his accident could easily have ended his life. For a long time, a feeling of dread prevented him from getting onto the bike that nearly killed him. But he finally garnered the courage, and today he cycles 130 kilometres every weekend and has completed 22 Cape Town Cycle Tours.

His concluding remark is food for thought: 'If Nick Vujicic could become such a global icon despite being born without arms and legs, the rest of us have no excuse not to get up each day – as early as 5 am! – visualise success and reach for the sky.'

CRAIG MILLER

A shy guy's journey to the JSE Top 10

— INTERVIEW: JUNE 2021 —

As a student at Norkem Park High School in Kempton Park, Johannesburg, the introspective Craig Miller could not think of anything worse than a career that would require expressive writing and public speaking. It chased him into the numerical arms of accounting, a career he believed would afford him and his calculator serenity and solitude.

But as they say, life is what happens to you while you're making other plans. As finance director of Anglo American Platinum, the world's largest producer of platinum-group metals, he accepts that regular and effective communication with employees, investors and host communities is now a part of his daily job. Although experience and training have helped Craig overcome his natural reticence to being in the public eye, he remains an introvert who prefers not to draw too much attention to himself.

Craig matriculated in 1991 and pursued a Bachelor of Accounting Science degree through the University of South Africa. He undertook vacation work at Deloitte in Johannesburg during his studies and joined the accounting firm after graduating in 1995. On completion of his training contract in 1998, Craig was enlisted into Deloitte's Global Development Programme, which took him to the London office a year later.

Anglo American Platinum's Craig Miller *(Photo: Geoff Brown)*

ON THE PLATINUM PATH

While in the United Kingdom, Craig was introduced to the world of mining when he was deployed to audit the Anglo American conglomerate. The assignment altered his long-held ambition of becoming an audit partner: he found the work environment very appealing; the culture was professional; the people had an admirable work ethic; and the systems were first class.

His opportunity to formally join the company came in 2000 when he was offered the position of financial manager responsible for financial reporting. He accepted without a moment's hesitation.

Craig had another life-changing encounter in London, when he was introduced to a striking young South African teacher called Nina. He won her over with his shy charm and persuaded her that the notion of a lifetime together was a prodigious idea. They moved back to South Africa in 2001 and got married three years later.

'On my return to Joburg, I joined Anglo American Coal as the finance person involved in various acquisitions and capital projects,' Craig recalls. 'I also undertook business development activities in Colombia, Venezuela and Australia, which required me to travel to some interesting and remote parts of the globe. In 2005, I was promoted to CFO and one of the most memorable transactions I worked on during that time was a significant black economic empowerment deal.'

BECOMING A RIGHT-HAND MAN

In 2007, the group's Executive for Human Resources approached Craig with an offer to head the office of the new Anglo American plc Group CEO in London. At the time, the CEO position was newly filled by Cynthia Carroll, not only the first non-South African but also the first woman to head the group. Her business acumen led to her being listed on *Fortune* magazine's International Power 50 index in 2008, and *Forbes* magazine ranked her the fifth most powerful woman in the world in 2009.

For Craig, working with Cynthia was a 'phenomenal experience'. It was fulfilling to work side by side with the chief executive of a company with 168 000 employees and operations in 45 countries. He got to understand first-hand the complexities of leading a major diversified mining company, and to witness the workings of a board made up of some of the world's best business leaders. The role enabled him to network with the leadership of the constituent companies and the relationships he built have proven to be incredibly valuable in the two decades he has worked for the group.

Some would argue that Cynthia's tenure at Anglo American was characterised by a number of jaw-dropping moments, one of which was an unprecedented move in the company's platinum business that signalled a bullish but necessary step to walk the talk when it comes to safety in the workplace. Two months after she took over, she shut down the company's mining operations in Rustenburg to conduct safety training. The Rustenburg site – which, at the time, reported an average of more than 45 deaths annually – was one of the cornerstones of the group and employed more than 20 000 employees. Although the shut-down cost the group millions of dollars and many commentators openly called her crazy, Cynthia's non-negotiable stance led to a drastic improvement in safety performance and has left a lasting positive legacy at Anglo American and in the South African mining industry.

'A lot of things have been written and said about Cynthia, most of which is contrary to my experience of working with her,' says Craig. 'She was often very demanding – as any good leader can be. But I think that came with the job, as she was under immense pressure to deliver. To me, she was incredibly professional and very appreciative of the work I did. I admired her composure; at times that I found myself extremely dismayed about a situation, she, on the other hand, would be quite calm and focused, despite what the consequences would be for her and the company.'

BABIES, BRAZIL AND BACK TO BRITAIN

In July 2009, Craig decided to return to South Africa to take up a CFO role in the ferrous and industries division. A few months later, Nina gave birth to their twin boys. Just as they were settling down to life as parents, Craig was offered the opportunity to take up the role of CFO of Anglo American Iron Ore in Brazil. The couple and their four-month-old babies moved to Rio de Janeiro in early 2010.

He is grateful to Nina for taking breaks in her career to accompany him on international assignments, particularly the stint in Brazil. Neither of them spoke a word of Portuguese before they got there but Nina took it in her stride. 'She has been incredibly understanding and gracious,' Craig reflects. 'I definitely would not be where I am without her support.'

The Minas-Rio iron ore project was identified as a major strategic growth initiative. Anglo American obtained control of the project in July 2008 and one of Craig's most pressing assignments when he arrived in Brazil was to support the construction of the world's longest iron concentrate pipeline. This was an integrated system comprising an open-pit mine, a beneficiation plant, a 529-kilometre pipeline, and an export terminal at the Atlantic port of Açu.

The undertaking brought a number of hurdles. Brazil is a federation, and with the pipeline traversing two states, each with its own regulations, the project was complex. As a completely greenfield project, it was projected to cost approximately US$3.5 billion and take three years to complete; in the end it took seven years and cost more than double the initial budget.

In October 2014, tears of joy welled in Craig's eyes when the company announced the delivery of 'first ore on ship'.

'I was on my way to the Middle East to see a customer when I got the message,' Craig says. 'It was disappointing not to be there to witness it myself, but I enjoyed watching the video of our team ringing the bell to signal that the *Key Light* bulk carrier vessel had been successfully loaded. It meant that a project that took so long and cost so much was finally complete and ready to undertake delivery of high-quality iron ore product for decades to come.'

In 2015, Craig was appointed group financial controller of Anglo American and returned to London. But it was to be a testing time. Depressed commodity prices meant a few difficult decisions had to be made on the operational side. As financial controller, he worked with the corporate finance department to identify areas where the group could reduce costs. Given that over 70% of costs related to wages and salaries, this unfortunately meant many people had to lose their jobs. 'That was the lowlight of my career. The retrenchment exercise really hurt,' Craig laments.

MANAGING CRISES

His job has come with a number of difficulties. For one, travelling around the world meant that he couldn't spend as much time with his family as he would have wished. The Miller family finally returned home to South Africa in 2019, when Craig took up his current position.

He describes it as the highlight of his career so far, as it requires him to use all the skills he's had to build along the way, including effective communication and technical financial expertise. Craig quickly learnt that the role of finance involves not onlypreparing accurate and credible numbers but also communicating these in a manner that is understandable to those who are not financially inclined, to help them grasp the significance of the underlying issues.

'I've been through many different scenarios that have prepared me for this job, including an expensive capital project, working for joint ventures and sitting on company boards,' Craig explains. 'I feel very blessed to come into this role with this level of preparation.'

His preparation has surely been put to the test since he took on the CFO role.

Craig relates how the newly rebuilt phase A unit of their converter plant in Rustenburg was damaged in February 2020 after an explosion during start-up proceedings. 'The phase B unit was commissioned to take over, but then a water leak was detected in the unit. Subsequent to repairing the leak, another, unrelated water leak was detected'. As water in a furnace can cause an explosion, the phase B unit had to be taken offline for repairs, leading to a complete halt in production for several weeks and forcing the company to declare *force majeure* on its contracted deliveries.

These challenges had a significant impact on the financial results Craig is responsible for. To make matters worse, the world was hit by the COVID-19 pandemic, with South Africa imposing a strict lockdown in March 2021.

'When the lockdown announcement was made, I remember sitting at my desk before joining a business continuity call and wondering how on earth we were going to get through this on top of the converter plant issue we were dealing with at the time. I was thinking to myself: "How long will it last and what should we do? What will the future look like?"

'I decided then, and still believe now, that the answers lie in being honest with ourselves. We've never had to deal with something like this before and we do not have all the answers. But if we work together, we'll get through it.'

Craig believes a key thing about getting through a crisis is understanding that it will always come to an end. It is important to develop resilience and the ability to pre-empt the unexpected. This includes recognising that such events should not be taken personally.

Being in an industry that experiences fluctuating prices and witnessing the impact of being financially overstretched, Craig believes that disciplined capital allocation and an appropriate and sustainable level of gearing and sufficient liquidity are important to handle the shocks when they come along.

'I would add that the best way to work through tough times is to tackle them as a team. Collaboration and transparency go a long way. Letting everybody know what exactly the situation is helps develop a common understanding of the issue and what the plan to resolve it is. A problem spread among many is often easier than one spread among only a few.'

STRATEGY AND MANAGEMENT APPROACH

The challenges the company has experienced have led them to adapt their strategy. The focus is now on ensuring resilience to external shocks while at the same time investing in future prospects that would grow the business. According to Craig, a good strategy strikes a balance between focusing only on what can realistically be achieved and being flexible and ambitious enough to grasp opportunities when they materialise. The strategy needs to take into account the macro- and socio-economic environment in which the company operates, set out key milestones and staggered delivery objectives, and result in greater value for shareholders.

'We also recognise that the business environment in South Africa has changed and there is now even greater need to work closely with our host communities, government and other stakeholders to create shared value. We want our stakeholders to view us as a valuable partner, rather than just this thing that sits on a hill close by.'

'Despite the impact of the coronavirus and the converter plant breakdowns, the company managed record headline earnings – R46 billion – in 2021. There are very few companies enjoying this kind of success and my view as finance director is that we need to be responsible with what we do with such profits. This includes being balanced in how we allocate capital and financial resources, supporting our employees, our communities and government as we tackle the pandemic and delivering financial returns to our shareholders.'

Craig is sometimes referred to as 'Dr No' in the business because of the firm stand he has to take in ensuring expenditure is sensibly managed. In doing so, he tries to have a management style that lends itself to guiding rather than directing people.

'I try to encourage people to think for themselves and to explore ideas they ordinarily wouldn't have considered in performing their duties. I also find that collaboration in a team is more effective than one-on-one instructions. As a result, we celebrate successes as a group much more than we do as individuals.'

In light of his management style, Craig is drawn to people who are team players when recruiting individuals for or promoting them in the finance function. One of Anglo American's values is care and respect, alongside safety, innovation, collaboration, accountability and integrity. It is important that employees have a similar value system to that of the company, something Craig says he can pick up on quite quickly.

'Beyond that, I think a good staff member is one who is ambitious and works hard. I recognise that not everybody wants to be the CEO or CFO, but it is still vital for employees to be motivated to go one step further and be determined to do better. One should have a level of professionalism that produces work that results in good outcomes ... work they can be proud of.

'Finally, I always try to have diversity of thought and perspectives in my team, as broad ideas give birth to the most robust solutions.'

LESSONS FOR ASPIRING FINANCE MANAGERS

Craig remembers his mom often saying that 'what is for you will not go past you'. He shares this wisdom with young professionals and advises them to grab every opportunity that comes their way and to develop resilience and confidence as early as possible in their careers. It is more important to focus on broadening your knowledge and horizons than to aim to climb the corporate ladder. The latter is a natural consequence of the former.

'Early in your career, you should focus on chasing experience rather than positions. I've had opportunities for further promotion twice, but turned them both down. While they would have been fruitful at the time, I would have stagnated and not have progressed much further. The biggest growth opportunity for me was moving out of finance into the CEO's office. I could have stayed in the finance function, but there is no way I would have learnt the professional and personal aspects I did or developed the network that has helped my career further down the line.'

Hard work pays off, but for Craig it is also important to find a balance between work and family life. As Jesse Jackson once said, 'children need your presence more than your presents'.

'If there is one aspect of my career I would change, it would be how much time I previously spent with my family. I often wonder what kind of childhood my sons would remember. Would they think of their dad as someone who was around a lot or as a figure consumed by his job?'

One of the few positive corollaries of the pandemic is that working from home has become the norm for many. This has enabled Craig to spend much more time with Nina and their pre-teen boys.

At the time of our interview, the day after Youth Day 2021, he is at their holiday home in Knysna. He mentions how the day before he and his wife had a conversation with their boys about the meaning of Youth Day.

'We also reflected on the book *To Kill a Mockingbird* by Harper Lee. It shares a major theme with one of the books the boys were doing at school, *Born a Crime*, by Trevor Noah, namely the impact of hatred and prejudice and not to judge a book by its cover. I've found this lesson to be very valuable in my career and particularly being able to empathise with people. We should all have an appreciation for people's background and experiences before making decisions about them.'

As we end the interview, I ask Craig whether he sees himself as CEO of Anglo American Platinum one day. 'People often ask me that, given that I usually fill in for our CEO, Natascha Viljoen, when she's on leave. Sometimes I think it would be great to be appointed to the role but other times I think to myself, "Goodness! Are you kidding me!?"

'For now, I feel very honoured to be the CFO of a Top 10 company on the JSE [Johannesburg Stock Exchange] and proud of the contribution we make in South Africa. I believe my current role gives me the best of both worlds, because I get to participate in critical strategic business decisions while having a firm hand on the financial pulse of the company.'

FATHIMA GANY

Cancer survivor with a new definition of work

— INTERVIEW: JULY 2021 —

Fathima Gany grew up within the confines of a small and insular Muslim community in the Indian suburb of Shallcross in Durban. Her interactions were limited to the inhabitants of her street, many of whom were her relatives. The education of women was not a major priority in her community, but Fathima always yearned for greater independence and to learn more about the world.

Her family did not permit her to register at a residential university, but she was allowed to do a correspondence course and enrolled for the accounting course at the University of South Africa. Upon completing her degree in 1997, she got an articles contract with Ernst & Young in Durban. Her family was apprehensive about her taking the job, because it was uncommon for Muslim women to join the corporate workplace at the time.

She told them that she would be back, ready to get married, after doing her three years of training. Twenty-two years later, she is yet to return from the workplace.

SETTING OFF INTO THE WORLD

Joining Ernst & Young was a major culture shock for the innocent girl from Shallcross. She not only had to get used to taking the bus

Cast Products' Fathima Gany *(Photo: Saijil Singh)*

from Shallcross to 320 West Street in the central business district – a 46-kilometre round trip – but also needed to adapt to conventions like using a knife and fork, as members of the Muslim community usually eat with their hands. Fathima also had to learn to distinguish between an Afrikaner and an Englishman, a Zulu and a Xhosa.

Her world was turned upside down, but the profound desire to learn about life beyond Shallcross led her to embrace it with open arms. She even attended mass at a colleague's church just to better understand other religious beliefs. 'We may be diverse, but we are all the same; we're all human at the end of the day,' she explains.

In meeting and getting to know new people, Fathima blossomed like a flower that had been touched by rays of the resplendent sun. In contrast, the auditing profession was not something she took a liking to. She found 'ticking and bashing' an incredible bore and hankered for a better grasp of the business process.

In 2001, Ernst & Young seconded her to act as financial manager at Veolia Water, and she joined that company on a permanent basis six months later. Veolia is a French waste, water and energy solutions company that went through a series of acquisitions at the turn of the century. In 2002, Veolia purchased Chematron and Fathima was made the general manager of administration and finance for this subsidiary, which also meant she had to move to Johannesburg.

'When I joined Chematron, we had a turnaround strategy for the business as it was not cash sustainable. It was a steep learning curve coming out of an audit environment, where all we did was ask questions and document answers. Suddenly I was charged with negotiating with banks for funding and managing supplier payments. As a project company, the cash flows were lumpy rather than steady and this made cash management even more challenging.'

In 2003, Fathima was appointed CFO of Veolia Southern Africa, where she got to work with a 'fantastic' CEO by the name of Gunter Rencken. 'Every time he picked up a pen and started drawing on his white board, I knew I was about to learn something. I'm really indebted to him for helping me learn the ropes in my first gig as a CFO.'

Gunter equally enjoyed working with the novice CFO. 'From our very first interaction working together, I could tell she had immense potential, despite her youth,' Gunter says. 'I liked that, unlike many CFOs who are obsessed with compliance, she had an entrepreneurial approach and would think innovatively about finding solutions. We had many healthy debates, and she was open to correction and new ideas. As CEO, I relished having her as a sounding board.'

Veolia was a start-up when Fathima joined, but grew significantly through acquisitions across sub-Saharan Africa. Working for a new company that undergoes substantial growth in a short period is a great career experience, as one is at the forefront of establishing systems, recruiting people and integrating acquisitions. 'I was so busy – the six years I spent at the company flew past!' Fathima says.

As Veolia was a French company, Fathima realised that employees who were conversant in French were in a better position to thrive there. Not wanting to be limited by this, she left the company in December 2007 to become the marketing planning manager at Yum! Brands, the franchise holder for KFC, Taco Bell and Pizza Hut. Yum was a fantastic organisation to work for, she says. She liked that it was people oriented and it had an amazing culture. Working with Nikki Rule, the marketing officer, taught Fathima about various marketing concepts, such as consumer behaviour, living standard measures and spending power.

'Everyone who works at Yum is happy to be there – and it is not just because of the free food,' Fathima laughs. 'I had no plans of leaving so soon, but eight months into the role, I was head-hunted to become the CFO of Insimbi, which is listed on the JSE [Johannesburg Stock Exchange]. It is quite a prestigious thing to be the finance director of a company on the stock exchange and therefore I decided to take up the offer effective September 2008.'

CFO OF A LISTED COMPANY

Insimbi used to be an owner-managed business, but now needed controls to be implemented, as well as the right processes to ensure compliance with JSE listing requirements. This, coupled with managing investor relations, was a new field for Fathima but it offered yet another learning opportunity.

However, she was not involved in the commercial side of the

company, which was something she had become accustomed to at Veolia. She missed that aspect of her previous roles and this made her consider other opportunities. In early 2011, she took up the position of CFO at Westcon Southern Africa, which promised strong business partnering opportunities. Westcon is a distributor of ICT products and, and a subsidiary of Datatec, listed on both the JSE and the London Stock Exchange. Although this was a new industry for Fathima, she could fall back on her experience at Veolia in executing mergers to oversee a series of acquisitions at Westcon while she was the finance leader.

'When people think about acquisitions, they usually think in terms of the actions that precede a merger, like due diligence and valuations. But the real deal is the integration subsequent to the transaction. The most demanding part of bringing businesses together involves change management, preserving existing value, choosing a corporate identity and aligning people, policies and processes My involvement in this work was very fulfilling,' she says.

In late 2013, Fathima was invited for a meeting with Ian Maclean, the Southern Africa CEO of the multinational engineering firm Parsons Brinckerhoff. She thought that the company was looking for a non-executive director to sit on their board, but she was in for a surprise. After meeting the other members of the board, I received an offer to become the CFO of the company. I didn't see that coming because none of our discussions were centred around managing the accounting department.'

Maclean explained that he was not looking for a traditional CFO; they already had a finance function that worked perfectly fine. They were looking for a CFO with strong relationship expertise to deal with issues such as long-outstanding debt, which should be handled by a senior director rather than a debtor's clerk. They wanted someone who could liaise with big company treasuries and capital committees for business development and financial contract management, Fathima recalls.

ADVENTURES AT PARSONS BRINCKERHOFF

Fathima took up the challenge in February 2014 and she found in Parsons Brinckerhoff a company that was involved in turnkey projects, most of which were funded by the World Bank. As CFO, she had to have regular conversations with the funder for business development purposes.

The company also had several subcontracting arrangements with Eskom while the Medupi power plant was being constructed. As procurement agents, they had to ensure that the completed works were satisfactory, and the corresponding pricing was on an arms-length basis. This resulted in occasional threats, some involving gunmen, that necessitated round-the-clock security for Fathima and her fellow Parsons Brinckerhoff executives.

'Every morning I wake up and pray for grounding. In this job, the temptation to compromise on your values will always be there. At the end of the day, nothing is more important than your reputation, and your reputation is defined by whether you abide by your ethics and retain your integrity.'

In late 2014, WSP acquired Parsons Brinckerhoff and Fathima ended up working for CEO Mathieu du Plooy, who was in charge of WSP in Africa. She has great respect for both Ian Maclean and Du Plooy because they let her apply her core competencies to her role without interfering. This included integrating the two businesses, harmonising remuneration scales and establishing a common enterprise resource planning system.

'Fathima is good at executing strategy,' Du Plooy says. 'All you need to do is explain to her where we are and where we want to go, and she will find a way of making it happen. She pays close attention to detail and takes ownership of work assigned to her. She is supportive of her team and is incredibly driven.'

The merger meant that Parsons Brinckerhoff executives had to leave the combined business, because WSP came with their own management team. Fathima stayed much longer than initially expected because Du Plooy wanted her to continue managing the key accounts she was responsible for, including Eskom.

However, in May 2017 she joined Cummins Inc. as CFO for the Africa–Middle East region. 'I am not surprised Fathima chose to leave,' Du Plooy confesses. 'She is the kind of CFO who thrives where there is a challenge, like turning entities around or integrating businesses after a merger. She easily gets bored once a business settles down to routine activities.'

LIVING OUT HER LIFE PURPOSE AT WORK

Working at Cummins was different from her previous experiences, as it is an American Fortune 500 company. It has a complex hierarchy with different verticals, ranging from subject matter experts to regional heads, all reporting to Fathima. One of the main reasons the company wanted Fathima was her experience in enterprise resource planning, which was to come in handy as they migrated to a new system. She also took charge of attending to internal and external audit matters, which required much of her attention.

'At Cummins, I worked with a really great group of people,' Fathima says. 'I would have stayed longer but for my father's advice. Going with Prophet Muhammad's life as an example, my father often said that the first 42 years of your life are to find your purpose, the next 20 years are to live your purpose, and anything beyond that is a bonus for which you should be grateful to your creator.'

Fathima believes her purpose in life is to serve in a job that puts people first. She decided to join Cast Products as CFO in November 2020, since the role would require her to assist in the turnaround of a business that was in financial trouble. During the interview process, she came to understand that the company was central to a value chain that involved 10 000 jobs. Saving the company was therefore pivotal to the livelihoods of so many people.

'I've been here for nine months now, and it's not been easy,' Fathima says. 'I'm the only executive on site, as the CEO is based in America and only visits from time to time. I have sleepless nights and sometimes I wake up dreading going to work. But I go in for the simple reason that I understand what the end goal is – saving jobs. It will take time, but I truly believe we will be successful.'

Fathima's advice for professionals is to 'safeguard their brand'. Your intellectual property comprises many things, including your academic background, your training and your experience. But the paramount component is your reputation, she believes. 'People will hire you, seek your opinion and ultimately ask you to sit on their board of directors if your brand is impeccable.

'If you were to phone any of the people I've worked with, they would probably say I'm an interesting character. But they will hopefully end the conversation by saying positive things about me. I don't believe that there is a grey area when it comes to integrity; I always stand for what is right. Finance goes beyond the numbers; it is about being a good corporate citizen.'

Fathima also advises professionals to keep learning because 'the point at which you stop seeking knowledge is the point at which you cut off your oxygen supply'.

'If ever you're faced with more than one option for a job, always pick the one that makes you feel most uncomfortable, because that's the job that will teach you the most. It will also test your resilience and help you grow,' Fathima says.

'It is not just learning that one should pursue, but also unlearning,' she continues. 'I served articles in the nineties, so many of the things I was taught are outdated in the modern world. I need to unlearn them and create mental space to embrace new thinking. The same applies to societal biases, which most of us have and that we need to shake off. And as you learn, you also need to teach, because leadership entails helping other people grow.'

Finally, Fathima advises up-and-coming professionals to understand that work is not your livelihood; it is only a means to your livelihood. She learnt this in beating cancer during the time she was at Cummins. When the chips were down, it was her close friends and family who frequently visited and checked on her, she says.

'Looking back, I regret the many periods that I was too busy working to spend time with my child and my parents. Achieving a work–life balance, where you give work and family the same amount of time, is difficult. But ensuring your family always know that they are loved and appreciated can help you to achieve work–life integration.'

MICHAEL MICHAEL

The finance of rare finds

— INTERVIEW: JUNE 2021 —

I first met Michael Michael in 2005 when I was an auditing clerk at RSM Betty & Dickson in Johannesburg. He was a senior partner at the firm and I was in trouble with him quite a few times. What I didn't know then but realised later was that we were similar in at least one respect: Michael was also not particularly keen on auditing and often procrastinated when it came to reviewing audit files.

While I was still biding my time as a clerk, he was asked to meet with Kevin Burford, a potential client. It turned into an opportunity to leave auditing. At the time, Burford was the financial director of Gem Diamonds and they needed assistance listing on the London Stock Exchange (LSE).

Although Michael's experience with such engagements was limited to South Africa, he managed to convince Kevin that he was the right man to help the company meet the requirements to have an initial public offering on the LSE's alternative investment market (AIM). He did such an admirable job that he was asked to leave RSM and join Gem on a permanent basis as group financial manager.

'Executing that listing in 2007 was one of the highlights of my career,' Michael says. 'We were initially meant to list the company on AIM, the market for smaller upcoming companies, but the shareholders

Gem Diamonds' Michael Michael *(Photo: Gem Diamonds)*

decided to go for a listing on the main board of the LSE. Attaining the public offering on that board was an incredible achievement for a one-year-old company.'

That year, 2007, yielded both good news and bad news for Gem Diamonds. The listing on the LSE was followed by the onset of the global financial crisis. The world changed practically overnight when the financial system went into distress, triggering a credit crunch. This brought severe liquidity constraints and put the company's management under pressure to meet debt obligations. The situation was worsened by the price of rough-cut diamonds declining by about 70%.

'The global financial crisis hit us very hard!' Michael recalls. 'There was a real fear that the company would not make it. We had to do an emergency capital raise to get funds to meet our obligations. I remember us sitting by our phones at 11 pm on 31 March 2008 waiting for our lenders to approve the payment plan. It was quite a relief that they did.'

Gem Diamonds' share price dropped by 75% in 2008, forcing the company to change strategy. They sold their interest in the Democratic Republic of Congo and placed their mines in Indonesia, Botswana, the Central African Republic and Angola under 'care and maintenance'. This term is used in the mining industry to refer to the process of ceasing production and maintaining a site in a manner that will allow mining to restart at a later stage.

In 2010, the company was helped by a rebound in rough and polished diamond prices. The Letšeng mine in Lesotho sold three exceptional white diamonds, which helped return the company to profitability. The company disposed of their Australian Ellendale mine in 2012 and embarked on development of the Ghaghoo mine in Botswana.

APPOINTMENT AS GROUP CFO

In 2013, Burford retired from the company and Michael was appointed as his replacement. In his first year as CFO, good financial results allowed the company to pay its maiden dividend to shareholders.

Michael's role involves formulating and implementing strategies that ensure good results are consistently delivered. 'At the end of the day, your strategy needs to be geared towards creating wealth. This does not just mean financial prosperity, but wealth in every sense of the word. It includes developing and growing employees, uplifting communities and creating value for shareholders. The strategy needs to consider all players across the value chain.'

The best strategies are those that anticipate opportunities which may not be apparent at the time when the plan is being set out. In the current depressed economic environment, it is tempting for Gem Diamonds to go into survival mode and 'hide under the covers' until the storm has passed, Michael says. But that would be a mistake, he believes, as there are prospects that can be taken advantage of.

'For example, there are organisations and mining assets that are in distress, which a well-funded company could seek to take over. While some may see it as preying on the weak, we don't. We see it as finding a win-win solution for entities that would otherwise go bankrupt or remain under care and maintenance for a long time without the ability to restart operations.'

Technology is also an important cog in the strategic wheel. This is particularly true for the diamond industry.

'Unlike with other minerals, no two diamonds are the same. The pricing is also not linear: the price of a five-carat diamond will not be five times that of a one-carat stone. The price will be much higher, depending also on the quality. As a result, we need the kind of technology that will cause the least damage to our diamonds during extraction and production.'

The company has seen the benefits of investing in first-class mining technology. In 2018, they recovered the 910-carat Lesotho Legend, which sold for US$40 million. Two years later, in October 2020, a 439-carat diamond, christened the Letšeng Icon, sold for US$16 million.

Strategy is a long-term process that requires short-term decision-making mechanisms to steer the business through different cycles, says Michael.

'When your business is operating well and generating cash, it's easy to be fixated on longer-term goals, forgetting that a crisis may come along that will force you to treat survival as your primary concept. You always need to keep an eye on emerging and principal risks to be ready for possible headwinds.'

HANDLING THE COVID-19 CRISIS

Michael coughs intermittently during our interview as he is recovering from COVID-19. His entire family got infected and Michael is thankful they all recovered without needing hospitalisation.

'This pandemic has been quite stressful, both personally and professionally, but I'm thrilled with how we worked as a team. I can say without fear of contradiction that not a single person at Gem rested on their laurels while we were working from home without supervision. As staff, we also took the extra step of sacrificing part of our salaries to ensure that there was sufficient liquidity to keep the company going.'

The diamond trade was impacted by the global pandemic in that access to Belgian, Indian and Israeli markets was limited owing to import and export suspensions. This led to a slowdown in sales for Gem Diamonds. In Lesotho, where the company's primary diamond-producing mine is based, the government implemented a 30-day lockdown at the start of the second quarter of 2020.

'Whereas in the corporate environment it's easy for people to shut down their laptops and retreat to their home offices, it's much more complicated for a mining operation. We had 1 500 people working at Letšeng in a controlled environment with regular testing and health protocols, who suddenly had to leave for their homes in the rural areas. This presented safety and logistical concerns.'

The pandemic was like the global financial crisis in that it presented liquidity challenges, with the company unable to make sufficient sales to meet their obligations. This resulted in Gem Diamonds relying on *force majeure* clauses in contracts with suppliers and having to negotiate with financiers. On top of that, the company had to spend US$1 million to contain the spread of COVID-19.

'The CFO worked very closely with our funders to ensure the group's debt structures remained resilient, efficient and appropriate,' Gem Diamonds' chair, Harry Kenyon-Slaney, writes in the Annual Report for 2020.

Together with other players in the mining sector, Gem Diamonds convinced the Lesotho government that they could resume operations safely. But restarting a mining operation is not as simple as flipping a switch, and it took two months to regain full production. It was a challenging time for the company's leadership team, having to decide on possible staff retrenchments and cancelling supplier contracts.

Yet the company ended up having one of its most profitable years ever after the market made an unprecedented recovery. Gem Diamonds saw an 83% increase in its profit after tax from continuing operations and declared its first dividends to shareholders for several years. No employees were retrenched, and suppliers were also duly compensated.

According to Michael it's teamwork that gets a company through a crisis like the COVID-19 pandemic. 'It's about everybody getting onto the matter, understanding the challenges and working closely together to find solutions. You also need to be proactive and address the issue early on. If you had kept abreast of world issues, you would have known a pandemic was gathering steam across the world and would have taken steps to attend to potential risks.'

GOOD EMPLOYEE TRAITS

Michael advises young professionals to look for something positive in every situation, rather than reading too much into the different scenarios they find themselves in.

'Sometimes new employees are no different from my children,' Michael says. 'For example, if my daughter sends a text message to a friend, and the friend doesn't respond within a few minutes, she'll complain about being "blue-ticked". She immediately assumes her friend has ignored her, yet the friend could simply be busy and respond later. In the same way, I'd advise professionals not to always assume the worst, but to consider the alternatives that may help to explain different situations.'

Michael gets amused by his children, who at times complain about seemingly insurmountable challenges they have to face. 'I tell them these are first-world problems and things could be a million times worse. Similarly, at the office, I see people getting extremely frustrated about an issue when it's really not the end of the world. It's often totally unnecessary to feel so sorry for yourself over a certain state of affairs when there are people out there who would kill to be in your situation, given the unemployment rate we have in this country.'

It's crucial to be satisfied in your job, Michael says. 'You spend so much time working, time you also spend away from your loved ones. So it's imperative that you enjoy your work and feel you can have some fun.

'Beyond that, find a job that is challenging. Look for something that will make you uncomfortable so that you can learn new things and grow as an individual. There's no point in taking up a job that will not make you a better person by expanding your knowledge and enhancing your technical and professional skills.'

One of the key things Michael looks at when considering employees for promotion is how innovative they are. This does not mean that they should 'cook the books' in the financial reporting process, but rather that they should think of opportunities regardless of how simple the transaction is they're dealing with. They should also challenge decisions and offer their views, regardless of whether the organisation adopts them or not.

Fostering trust is another important aspect of building an effective team. The employee needs to trust the business, and vice versa. This provides a level of comfort that allows team members to be effective yet act with transparency and openness. A professional should therefore strive to earn the trust of the organisation.

MANAGEMENT STYLE

As our conversation comes to an end, I remind Michael of a dressing-down he gave me 16 years ago when I was a rather unmotivated first-year audit clerk at RSM. He caught me staring at a bird outside pecking at a generous bread crumb. I wished it was me outdoors, free from all the folders and files.

My daydreaming was interrupted by loud steps coming down the stairs, and a booming voice calling, 'Where the hell is KC?!'

'Here, sir,' I replied timidly.

'Listen here,' Michael said sternly. 'This will be the last time I remind you to submit your time sheet on time. Understood?'

'Yes, sir, it won't happen again,' I promised apologetically.

At the time Michael was the senior partner at the firm responsible for the time system. I was convinced he would fire me if I ever missed another deadline. A few weeks later, I was guilty of a much worse transgression.

It was mid-morning on a Friday and I had decided to begin my weekend *jol* a bit early by joining an online game. I was in one of the trickiest levels of the challenge and lost to the world, when I saw a hand tapping on my laptop. I swatted it away without looking up, thinking it belonged to one of my peers. The next moment I crashed out of the game and got up to moan at the person who had so rudely disrupted me. It was none other than Michael himself.

He calmly directed me to his office where he sat me down and gave me a lecture about abusing company resources and wasting company time. To this day I remain thankful that Michael was the forgiving kind, because he let me off the hook once again. In fact, a few hours later, we laughed about the incident over drinks at the company bar.

Michael responds with a hearty laugh when I recall these two incidents from our past. 'My management style has definitely changed over time. I've learnt that you have to stand back sometimes and give a platform to others. As a manager, it's not always easy to restrain myself from taking control, but I've realised there are talented people around me who have ideas that are often better than mine.'

He has learnt to delegate, which has given him more time for himself and has also helped with succession planning. 'I used to joke with my team, telling them that I'll be retiring in 2020 and that by then they should all be able to do each of my tasks. As a result, I have seen them grow by shadowing me, asking questions and learning new things.'

Despite corporate accountants always looking for greener pastures, Michael's core team has stuck with him for many years. It comes as no surprise: he is still the same nurturing and forgiving mentor I came to know when he counselled me in his office so many years ago.

DEON VILJOEN

Seeker of societal good

— INTERVIEW: AUGUST 2021 —

Deon Viljoen was one of the top science students at Hoërskool Edenvale on the East Rand, and on his way to pursuing a career in science. In 1982, his matric year, he was part of a select group of students who were invited to visit South Africa's nuclear research facility at Pelindaba to the west of Pretoria. But getting a glimpse of the kind of work he might be doing one day made him rethink his planned career choice.

He ended up in the numbers game on his father's advice, to consider becoming a chartered accountant, as the profession offered a stepping stone to several careers and industries.

'I didn't necessarily come from a family that can be described as well off in any way, but both my parents worked exceptionally hard to look after their three children and we were their absolute love and priority in life. That afforded me the opportunity of a university degree, for which I remain ever grateful,' says Deon.

At the time, he felt it his duty to contribute and the only way he knew how was through academic bursaries offered by the university. That meant a mere pass was not good enough as distinctions were needed to earn bursaries. 'Seeking distinctions in all my endeavours became my life motto and this has stood me in good stead throughout my career'.

Discovery's Deon Viljoen *(Photo: Discovery Marketing)*

He obtained his bachelor's degree cum laude in 1985 from the then Rand Afrikaans University (today the University of Johannesburg). After obtaining an honours degree from the same institution in 1986, he joined one of the predecessor firms of Coopers & Lybrand for articles the following year.

Back then, there was far less specialisation for article clerks in the big audit firms. Deon got to experience different industries and specialised in financial services only when he was sent on secondment to the Coopers & Lybrand London office in 1994. On his return to South Africa the following year, he became a partner in the Johannesburg Office and was instrumental in advancing the financial services specialisation within the firm.

'Audit firms were still true partnerships at the time,' Deon observes. 'This was a time when we considered each other partners and values like integrity and trust were nurtured in a very personal way. As firms become bigger and risks escalate, we've seen corporate culture inevitably creep in, with code of conduct becoming more formalised.'

In 1998, Coopers & Lybrand merged with Price Waterhouse to become PricewaterhouseCoopers (PwC) and Deon stayed on as a partner until February 2003. At that point he did a mid-career assessment. 'Although I truly enjoyed the profession, I asked myself whether I want to do the same thing until retirement. It would have been a valid career choice, yet I opted to take the leap and try something else before it was too late.'

BEING IN THE DRIVING SEAT

Deon joined Investment Solutions Holdings, an asset management subsidiary of Alexander Forbes. It was an opportunity 'to experience the other side of the desk, a chance to be in the driving seat when it comes to making financial decisions, rather than looking in the rear-view mirror, which is, to an extent, the role of the auditor.'

Not long after, in 2005, the then group CEO at Alexander Forbes, Rael Gordon, asked him to join the group's finance team to help tackle weighty matters at executive level. Deon is not one to shy away from a challenge. He grabbed the opportunity to move to the head office, where he worked with the 'very sharp and characterful' group CFO Mike Ilsley.

In 2007, there was an unsolicited bid by a consortium of private equity players to take the Alexander Forbes group private. Typical to private equity deals at the time, it was a leveraged buyout, with the group ending up with substantial debt as a result of the transaction.

'It was a complex transaction because the existing public shareholders wanted a vehicle through which they could still remain invested in the company,' Deon recalls. 'I took over as group CFO while the transaction was being implemented. Things got more complicated when, less than a year later, the global financial crisis hit, and the world was a distinctly different place.'

Despite his youthful appearance (he doesn't look a day older than 45), Deon says he aged in dog years during the stressful seven years that followed his appointment as CFO of Alexander Forbes in 2007. Managing the finances of a highly leveraged financial institution at a time when the global system was under severe pressure was not an easy undertaking.

'When you're in the doldrums, it always feels like the lowest point of your career. But when you look back at it, you realise how much you learnt and grew, and you become grateful for the experience.'

The company went through delisting from the Johannesburg Stock Exchange (JSE) in July 2007 and relisted on the bourse in 2014. While under the private equity consortium's control, the group underwent substantial strategic repositioning. Several subsidiaries were disposed of, and the group's strategic focus was narrowed. All these transactions required the active participation of the CFO, in that structures had to be put in place for working with the respective stakeholders, transaction advisers and auditors.

In 2015, Deon was declared CFO of the Year by CFO South Africa. At the awards ceremony, Trevor Hoole, then CEO of KPMG, described Deon as a 'person of integrity, a person of honour, someone to admire and emulate, someone of noble character and someone who has a sense of what is right'. It came as no surprise that when Edward Kieswetter resigned as Alexander Forbes CEO in February 2016, Deon acted as interim CEO until the new appointment later that year.

EXPLORING OTHER FIELDS

By early 2017, Deon had been with Alexander Forbes for over a decade, and he was ready for a different type of challenge. 'The opportunity to join Discovery came at the right time. After my initial discussions with Adrian Gore, the founder and CEO, I could not help but feel impressed by his vision and intellect. I was convinced that this role was the right fit for me because of the group's deeply entrenched purpose-driven approach, highly innovative culture and the brave initiatives they were undertaking, which included building a bank from the ground up.'

In May that year, Deon was appointed CFO of the Discovery group. What won Deon over was the group's proven track record and their shared-value model.

'The model works like this: A significant part of the financial value inherent in products such as health and life assurance is ultimately determined by the behavioural aspect of the insured, such as healthy lifestyle choices and physical activity. Considerable value can be unlocked if the client engages in healthy choices, and that value can be ploughed back into the relationship with the client, to continue driving a virtuous cycle. The same principles can be applied to, for example, driving behaviours in short-term insurance and financial behaviours in banking. At the same time, they also deliver substantial social good.'

Clients are encouraged, through an engagement programme and reward tiers, to alter their behaviour by doing things such as engaging in physical exercise, adopting safer driving behaviour, quitting smoking and saving actively. This leads to a reduction in risk and claims, which, in turn, translates into financial rewards for the client and monetary benefit for the group. These benefits are ploughed into investing in innovation, which ultimately leads to better products at lower premiums.

'In my view, this shared-value thinking was way ahead of its time and is exceptionally positioned for the future world. I was aware of it before, but its depth became more apparent only once I joined the company. It's an incredible environment to work in, very fast paced. The leadership is agile, and the people here are very talented.'

Deon believes that Discovery has some of the brightest people in corporate South Africa and whenever this team put their minds together, they formulate the best possible outcomes.

'As a company, doing what is right means identifying what our global differentiator is and leveraging it. Purpose, values and shared-value thinking are very much in the DNA of the company, from the leadership down to every staff member. We also prioritise benefit for the customer, as we strongly believe that not being able to promote a mutually beneficial relationship with your client will quickly make you irrelevant, particularly in the financial services sector.'

Deon believes his prior positions have been good training grounds for the challenges of his current position. 'Being appointed a partner at PwC was a career highlight for me because I got that position when I was relatively young. It was a defining moment, because it gave me a solid grounding for senior roles from then on. I was lucky enough to experience the challenges I did and there are choices I made along the way which have altered my career path.

'I'd like to think they were all the right choices, because I learnt a lot from them and continue to grow. I consider this a great privilege.'

STRATEGY

'While the business delivered a robust performance, the impact of the pandemic has been felt at every level of our Group,' Deon writes in the 2020 Discovery Integrated Annual Report. 'In addition to the direct health impacts of the virus, the operating context remains more uncertain than ever, with extreme volatility in interest rates and equity markets. For insurers, this meant that new business growth and increased lapses, as well as possible future claims, were under strain.'

He mentions that Discovery has had to respond in a deliberate and structured way to ensure that the group lives up to its responsibility as an insurer while making sure that the company remains solvent. They also had to strike a balance between stabilising their ship in choppy waters and keeping the promising new growth initiatives going.

'With a global pandemic such as COVID-19, there is no precedent to fall back on; the last time something like this happened, the world was a totally different place. We went back to our purpose of making people healthier and enhancing and protecting their lives. Because it is so ingrained in what we do, it came naturally, and our purpose and shared-value model have never been more relevant than during these unprecedented times. So, the lesson is that companies should be clear as to their purpose, embody good values and invest in good talent and technology, which can then be called upon in moments of crisis.'

Strategically, Deon advises leaders to understand where the world is moving to, trying to have a fairly good idea of how things will evolve. The future is not easy to predict, but the more information you gather, the easier it is to establish what will differentiate you from your competitors. Most importantly, your purpose should be clearly defined and embedded into the culture of your organisation.

'Discovery is a great example of visionary decisions made early on, which became more and more relevant over time. The group's purpose has hardly changed over time because it was futuristic from the beginning,' Deon says. 'We've enhanced and expanded it to different products, but the core has remained the same. The bottom line is getting your purpose and values to work in practice, rather than their simply being interesting words on a wall.

'We reviewed our values a while back and decided to add "force for social good" to the list because the idea was already so prominent in everything we do. The rest of our values stood the test of time because we've been living them from inception. Living your values enables you to remain ahead of the pack and to respond to environmental changes.'

ADVICE

Deon firmly believes that you should define yourself by who you are as a person rather than by what you do professionally. He may be the CFO of one of South Africa's biggest and most prestigious companies, but what is most important to him is living up to his responsibility in society, living with integrity and caring for his family.

'Professionals should not lose sight of the privilege they have to be professionals in a country where the unemployment rate and poverty levels are so high. It comes back to the shared-value idea: having such privilege makes it our responsibility to drive societal good. We can improve the solutions to societal problems if we put our minds together and it's up to each individual to figure out how they can participate in this.'

According to Deon it is important to distinguish between what is important to you personally and what is important to you professionally. You should have a personal purpose over and above your organisation's purpose so that you can stay true to yourself first. With that clarity of purpose, you should not hesitate to transfer your perspective to the organisation, because diversity of opinion is what makes an organisation stronger, he says.

Deon reminds young professionals that they need not fly alone when faced with challenges. Learn to identify when you need the input of others to get to a solution.

And, he says, have an eye for opportunities, so that you can seize them and drive them. In Deon's view, challenges should be seen as opportunities for growth.

'Never waste a good crisis – it's an opportunity for you to step up, learn and contribute,' he advises.

LERENA OLIVIER

Work hard, travel far

— INTERVIEW: MAY 2021 —

A writer doing background research can get quite a few insights from someone's social media pages. Take for example Lerena Olivier's Facebook page, which looks like a picture atlas and a love story. Happy images of Lerena and her husband, Wikus, show a couple truly content in each other's company as they explore the world, from Europe to what looks like the bright lights of the Big Apple. Her LinkedIn profile picture shows a genuine smile, like one borne from frequent use.

When I meet Lerena, my preconceived notions of her warm demeanour are immediately confirmed. She greets me as if we've known each other for years and we have the kind of light, natural conversation that you wish would go on forever.

I begin by asking her how she became an accountant.

'It happened by chance rather than by formal career guidance,' she recalls. 'My dad passed away when I was 18 and my mother was a housewife, so I did not have a career parent who could point me in the right direction when I matriculated. Because I was quite good at sciences, I thought chemical engineering might be the thing for me, so I paid a visit to a friend's dad who worked in the field.'

Once there, though, Lerena seemed to ask more questions about the six-month accounting curriculum included in the chemical engineering

Pick n Pay's Lerena Olivier *(Photo: Andrew Gorman)*

degree than about chemistry, which prompted her friend's dad to suggest accounting as a career. And so she ticked it as her first choice when she applied to Stellenbosch University.

After graduating with an honours degree in accounting in 1997, she joined Coopers & Lybrand (which later became PwC). Her main audit client during this stint was Shoprite, which introduced her to the inner workings of the retail industry. And she loved it.

'From the beginning I was quite taken with the industry because it involves direct interaction with consumers and tangible products. In addition, Shoprite had just acquired 139 OK Bazaars stores and kick-started the process of setting up a footprint elsewhere in Africa. I found the accounting around that quite interesting.'

Lerena joined Shoprite as a financial accountant in 2001. When the announcement was made in the company newsletter, many people came up to her saying they had always been under the impression she was already a Shoprite employee!

She spent a decade at Shoprite, rising to the position of group financial accountant. Her highlight was setting up the Training Outside Public Practice programme in the company, which enabled accounting graduates to undertake their articles through Shoprite's finance department. The programme grew from 10 trainees a year to 30 by the time Lerena left. This is something she is particularly proud of because she cares about talent development, especially for individuals from previously disadvantaged backgrounds.

'Another highlight was the team I had built up at Shoprite. We implemented system-based reporting, which simplified a very complex reporting process. Shoprite was in 19 countries by the time I left, with different teams and reporting processes that we needed to harmonise.'

The lessons learnt during her time at Shoprite include learning to rely on team members. 'Everyone has limitations as an individual and we need to be realistic about what we can do. It's tempting to want to solve every problem in front of you and to want to change everything at once. Colleagues may have different ways of doing things, which may take longer or follow a different route but also get the job done.'

She points out that having good systems in place takes away the need to micromanage staff, which is important for companies that have operations in different jurisdictions. Retail is a volumes business, with millions of transactions happening each month, and hence the need for effective controls cannot be understated.

MOVING TO PICK N PAY

In the autumn of 2011, Lerena was cold-called by a recruiter, asking whether she would be interested in taking up the role of Head of Reporting at the Pick n Pay group. Although she was not looking for another job, she decided it may be worthwhile to have a discussion with the then CFO, Bakar Jakoet. He wanted to modernise some of the group's reporting structures and was looking for someone who could assist in that process.

During their meeting, Jakoet presented a company with a long history and strong values, which immediately resonated with Lerena. Pick n Pay traces its origins back to the 1960s, when Raymond Ackerman purchased four stores in the Western Cape after being fired from Checkers, which is one of Shoprite's brands today. The Ackerman family have also become known for their opposition to apartheid, advocating consumer rights and supporting various charitable causes.

As the two largest supermarket brands in South Africa, there has always been healthy rivalry between Pick n Pay and Shoprite – and a staff member leaving one company for the other usually raises eyebrows. Lerena had to gather up all her courage before she could walk into her boss's office to break the news. But Marius Bosman, then managing director of Shoprite, was surprisingly understanding. He also asked whether there was anything he could do to convince her to stay.

'I told him that I saw this as a great growth opportunity and that I'd never use the offer as a tool to negotiate for a better salary. It was a difficult discussion, because he wanted me to reconsider my decision. However, after they got over the unexpected news of my leaving for the opposition, Marius and the entire company were quite supportive. It was a tearful parting after so many years at the company.'

On joining Pick n Pay, Lerena had the space to improve, innovate and grow. She was given the opportunity to lead the group finance team and to oversee the implementation of a system to automate the reporting process. The finance function also has a chartered accounting training programme, which Lerena has played a great part in growing.

'When I got here, the programme had only one trainee. Today we're taking in four trainees a year, mainly through the South African Institute of Chartered Accountants' Thuthuka initiative, which aims to increase the number of qualified black accountants. The programme trains a total of 12 trainees at any given time. I'm enthusiastic about talent development and it's wonderful to be at an organisation that shares this passion.'

EXECUTIVE APPOINTMENT

Jakoet retired from the CFO position at Pick n Pay in September 2019 and Lerena was appointed in his place. As an executive director of South Africa's second largest supermarket chain, Lerena plays an active part in formulating and executing big-company strategy.

'To craft a successful strategy, you must take yourself out of your day-to-day reality,' she advises. 'You need time away from the hustle and bustle to think. Our training as accountants emphasises linear thinking, where we're guided by set standards. This is good, because we need to ensure everything is within the tramlines. But we also need to think outside the box and have a cross-functional dimension in the plans we formulate for our businesses.'

As part of embracing constant change, you have to ask yourself if there are ways to do things better, Lerena says. This kind of thinking will unlock opportunities.

She feels that as an accountant, it is also important to understand the story behind the numbers. 'I tell my young accountants it doesn't help if they tell me the balance sheet is balanced. I need them to tell me what the balance sheet is telling them. In other words, how the balance sheet can be strengthened. This is how accountants can influence and drive the business while still fulfilling their "protector" role.'

As protectors, accountants are often obsessed with ideals such as containing costs. But this can end up slowing down the business and so one should also be agile and pragmatic. According to Lerena, rules are important but management needs to understand the reason for the rule. Changing a rule may have to be considered if it has become a deterrent to growth.

The kind of professionals Lerena seeks out to build a winning finance team are all self-starters. She believes it is important for team members to be driven and to enjoy what they do. Furthermore, she prefers colleagues who challenge her.

'It is also vital that we employ people who have the same values as the company. We are one of South Africa's biggest and most successful family-owned businesses, with family at the core of our values. This applies not only to our product offering for customers but also to how we operate in the company.'

Lerena believes that in the retail environment specifically a good team should consist of diverse individuals. A supermarket serves people from different backgrounds and as such the company should encourage different viewpoints within its ranks to satisfy the varied needs of its client base.

DEALING WITH DIFFICULTIES

When I ask her about dealing with conflict, she says it's important to avoid seeing yourself as a victim. For her, every situation offers an opportunity to grow, and you should always try to walk away a stronger person. When you encounter situations that appear to be unfair, she says you should act as a 'graduate of the Self-Esteem 101 class', with the ability to step aside and move forward.

The job of a listed-company CFO can be extremely stressful. There is nothing wrong with going to the bathroom and having a good cry when you are overwhelmed, Lerena says. 'You can then pull yourself together and come back to face the challenge. Women sometimes deal with pressured situations differently from their male counterparts, and while some perceive this to be a weakness, I see it as a strength. It is helpful to have a release valve rather than bottling up your emotions, which can be damaging to your well-being in the long run.'

Lerena also advocates compartmentalisation in moments of crisis. Breaking down a crisis into different components and tackling it bit by bit makes it more manageable than viewing the problem as a single wave, which can be too big to overcome when it makes landfall.

'Understanding the different parts of a problem is essential for its resolution,' she explains. 'Management should then determine which parts are a priority and which can be tackled later. The team should be clear on who needs to do what and by when.'

These are the principles that guided Pick n Pay's response to the COVID-19 crisis. Within three weeks, the company was able to let a majority of the support staff work from home by automating processes. The concept of teamwork was also vital in achieving continuity of operations in very uncertain times.

'We had to have our risk management department vet all changes to ensure that the new processes did not give rise to significant threats.

This was particularly important given that we have a national presence and government regulations were not uniformly applied across all provinces.'

As a supermarket chain, Pick n Pay was allowed to operate throughout the various lockdowns, except for intermittent restrictions on selling liquor, some general merchandise and clothing. Although remaining open for trade allowed the group to continue generating revenue, it presented challenges with regard to customer and staff safety. Effective communication had a significant role in ensuring expectations were understood and emerging issues were resolved. As a result, the group had one of its most resilient financial years in the annual period ended February 2021

LOOKING TO THE FUTURE

Lerena is looking forward to making a difference with her finance team. She is intent on making them a strategic partner to business operations. With the help of digitisation, the finance function is well placed to be an enabler and a value creator given that it has an overview of the entire business.

Lerena thinks her current role allows her to fully express her talents. She is particularly pleased about the opportunity to make a difference in people's lives, given her interest in people's development. 'I've always strived to find a way to do that in my career. In the future, I'd love to spend all my time uplifting people. This may ultimately be through a non-profit organisation.'

Other than spending time with family, Lerena loves to read. Because her daily life overflows with corporate and finance information, she prefers to read less weighty material in her free time. Her favourite author is Afrikaans writer Irma Joubert.

Apart from escaping with a good book, travelling the globe has been another way for her to truly get away from it all. But for a while her international travels had to be curbed because of global travel restrictions.

As someone who works hard and travels equally hard, she looks forward to a time when her Facebook page can finally be updated with adventures from Hamburg to Hanoi again.

LUVHENGO NESWISWI

Leading from the trenches

— INTERVIEW: OCTOBER 2021 —

As a pre-teen living in Soweto in 1987, Luvhengo Neswiswi once stumbled upon his father's payslip. He might still have been very young, but he knew enough of the world to be dumbstruck by the fact that their family of ten had to survive on the R180 per week his dad was earning as a van driver. From time to time, his mother supplemented the family income by selling traditional brew, but still, to say that they were an impoverished family would be to state the obvious.

So when Luvhengo started thinking of his future, the career choices he considered were driven by the desire to make as much money as possible and lift his family out of poverty. The few doctors he had seen in the community seemed to live fairly lavish lifestyles so Luvhengo set out to study medicine. Looking back, he realises this was quite ambitious given how poor the teaching in science was at Mavhungu Andries Secondary School in the former Venda homeland, where he studied at the time.

Then one day, as he was browsing through a copy of *The Sowetan*, he came across a job advertisement for a chartered accountant. The job paid a whopping R80 000 per year; it took Luvhengo some time to pick his jaw off the floor.

A job that paid ten times his father's salary? Whatever this thing was, he was going to become one!

CLIMBING THE CORPORATE LADDER

Luvhengo was sent to a rural secondary school in Venda because his parents believed he would be less distracted there than in the township of Soweto. Knowing they would not be able to put him through university, Luvhengo resolved to work hard to get a bursary. He was among the top achievers of the 1993 matric class in the Vuwani region.

Before getting a bursary from Deloitte to study accounting at the University of the Witwatersrand, he worked as a van assistant for the plastic manufacturing company where his father was employed. Luvhengo graduated with a Bachelor of Commerce degree in 1997, but did not pass his honours the following year. He joined Deloitte in 1998 and successfully completed accounting honours through correspondence study at the (now) University of KwaZulu-Natal.

Luvhengo qualified as a chartered accountant in early 2001 and was appointed as a manager at the audit firm later that year. He began looking for a different position in various entities and received offers from Citibank and the Mining SETA (Sector Education and Training Authority), neither of which appealed to him. In 2005, though, he was introduced to Tourvest CEO Tommy Edmond, who interviewed him for the role of head of finance at the tourism group. He took up the position of deputy CFO at Tourvest, passing up his pending appointment as a partner at Deloitte.

'Tommy and I had a deal,' Luvhengo recalls. 'I had two years to prove that I was capable of acting as the group's CFO. Jan Roesch, who was the CFO at that time, groomed me for the role, which I earned after eighteen months. I have been here ever since; I simply love this company because of its entrepreneurial flair.'

UPS AND DOWNS AT TOURVEST

Tourvest is a leading integrated tourism group, operating businesses that include travel management companies, hotels, lodges and restaurants, as well as craft, curio and jewellery shops and foreign exchange bureaux.

Luvhengo is not heavily involved in the financial reporting function of the business as he spends most of his time supporting the group CEO, Sean Joubert, in implementing strategy and capital allocation to projects

Tourvest's Luvhengo Neswiswi *(Photo: Agie Adams)*

that will yield maximum return for the group. The group prides itself on identifying and maximising opportunities, the best example being that of the hospitality business sprouting during the 2010 FIFA World Cup and becoming one of the group's most profitable ventures.

The COVID-19 pandemic has been a distinct low, having a devastating effect on all businesses in the travel and tourism sector. 'We've always identified viruses as a key risk to our businesses. But the models were based on past experiences with viruses such as Ebola, which had a local impact and affected only one segment of the group at a time. The coronavirus was a total shock, as all our activities simply ground to a halt, and we realised just how vulnerable our business is.'

Tourvest had expected to make a profit for the year ending 31 August 2020; instead, they suffered losses after collecting virtually no revenue for many months following the onset of the pandemic. This presented a significant challenge with regard to cash management, as expenses without corresponding inflows began depleting their cash reserves.

'We did all we could to avoid retrenching people, because our employees have a significant role in their communities. Most of our employees at tourism sites have more than one dependant. There usually are no other jobs in that area and so one retrenchment means long-term financial loss to a whole family. It breaks my heart that we had to cut close to half our workforce of 7 000, but it was necessary to save the company and to be in a position to create more jobs in the future,' Luvhengo explains.

The employees who have been retained have also had to take pay cuts, including the group's executives. With vaccination efforts increasing at the time of writing, and the world starting to learn to live with the virus, there is reason to hope that the end of the tunnel may be in sight.

At the time of our interview, Luvhengo was encouraged by travel restrictions starting to be relaxed, especially from Europe. 'Europe is a critical source market for our business, as 60% of inbound activity to our country comes from that continent. Being taken off the United Kingdom's red list also helped, as British travellers account for close to a fifth of all visitors to South Africa.'

CAREER LESSONS

When it comes to strategy, Luvhengo believes sustainability of a business should be the ultimate goal. In the tourism sector, this requires safeguarding the environment, which calls for green tours that protect the natural resources in the areas where they operate. That said, the CFO must also drive the profitability of the company, because no institution can survive in the long term with a negative bottom line.

The strategy should promote a culture that encourages people to thrive in their individual contexts. The collective benefit will become evident only if each person within the business has a sense of personal fulfilment. 'Our growth has been fuelled by the acquisition of businesses in the sector and integrating them. If we buy a business with the wrong culture, the likelihood of failed integration is very high and so our strategy is to avoid such acquisitions.'

Luvhengo also believes that a business should invest in innovation. Technology has changed things completely, and a business needs to move with the times or it will get left behind. As such, the group's strategy is designed to allocate capital to projects that incorporate technological advancement.

Luvhengo's advice to young professionals is to have a firm plan for what they want to achieve in life. Coming from a poor family, he needed to work hard because his parents did not have the funds to pay for his education, or the credit standing to get a loan. To help him stay the course when he was young, he wrote down affirmations that he read and reread as a reminder of what he wanted to achieve. 'If you have a clear vision in your life, you can always refer back to it when you experience challenges. This will help you keep focusing on the end goal, regardless of what you are experiencing at the time.'

Luvhengo learnt something quite profound from watching an interview with Warren Buffett, the American business magnate. He asked viewers to imagine walking up to view a painting of their life. It is something that takes years to paint, but what if it turns out to be something that you do not like or are not proud of? The lesson is this: as the driver of your own destiny, you can choose today what you want the picture to look like, so start to paint it how you want it to look one day.

'It's important for youngsters to know what they want, particularly now, because they have many more distractions than we had. You need to know where you want to go, because knowing that will allow you to head in the right direction even if you chose a different route along the way.'

Being an accountant can be very stressful, particularly in the commercial environment. Luvhengo encourages professionals to find ways of relieving stress. His release comes from running. To achieve good times, he needs to clear his mind of the issues he's dealing with. Going for a run revitalises him and prepares him to return to the 'shop floor'.

Switching off is an important part of dealing with stress. So, even at the height of the COVID-19 pandemic, he worked from the office so that he could switch off properly when he got home. He finds that focusing on work while in the office and focusing on family when at home he can give his best to both environments.

Regarding management, Luvhengo has learnt that teamwork is critical to survival, particularly in challenging times such as these. Another important element of good leadership is transparency: he believes management should be open with employees about the challenges the business faces, to help staff understand where the business is at and where it is headed. This will encourage them to go the extra mile to achieve a common purpose, including making sacrifices when required.

'Transparency goes beyond the company, because we also have to deal honestly with our suppliers. During the pandemic, this honesty helped us get favourable terms from the hundreds of landlords who host our businesses.'

Finally, a good leader is visible and accessible to the rest of the team. Being present in the office, chasing deadlines together, demonstrates to your team that you are with them in the trenches and leading from the front.

HANRÉ ROSSOUW

How a metallurgist became a master of money

— INTERVIEW: SEPTEMBER 2021 —

Of all the CFOs interviewed for this book, Sasol's Hanré Rossouw is the only one who is not a chartered accountant. In fact, he graduated in chemical engineering from Stellenbosch University. But Hanré has always wanted more, and his thirst for knowledge and new challenges would spur him on to gain other qualifications and experiences across a range of industries.

While his university friends spent their holidays learning to surf at Muizenberg, Hanré – who hails from Gqeberha – had to work at Anglo American as part of his bursary conditions. After he graduated in 1997, the company deployed him to Amcoal Colliery in Witbank (now eMalahleni), where he worked as a metallurgist. Hanré arrived with a degree from one of South Africa's top universities, only to find himself labouring as a shift worker, unloading coal from a train. At the end of each day, he had to scrub himself down with Handy Andy.

Yet he has fond memories of those days. Often, he would jump on the train and chat with the driver as the locomotive made its way towards the picturesque sunset of Mpumalanga's mining district. Talking to the drivers and mineworkers about their view of the country, their insights into mining and their life lessons was an experience he not only enjoyed but also learnt from.

Soon after joining Amcoal, Hanré realised that he was interested in more than just the technical aspects of the built environment. He wanted to understand the workings of business, and so enrolled for a Bachelor of Commerce degree through the University of South Africa. He graduated in 2001 and consequently decided to leave Anglo American because he believed it would take too long to rise through the ranks in engineering.

'I was young and in a hurry to conquer the world!' he says with a laugh. 'In early 2001, I joined Accenture as a strategy consultant. The transition was quite dramatic; on my last day at Anglo, I was outside in the sun, wearing overalls and a hard hat. The next day I was in a suit and tie walking into the air-conditioned hallway of the Bank of Lisbon for a treasury department analysis assignment.'

At Accenture, Hanré had banks and insurance companies as his primary clients. It was a great environment in which to learn about the ins and outs of commerce, as he was tasked with having to come up with ways of improving processes and determining which levers to pull to make businesses function optimally. He continued to build on the business knowledge he had gained at Anglo American in optimising production and conducting feasibility studies for new projects.

Hanré dealt a lot with change management, helping human resource departments to transform businesses. Coming from an engineering background, he had a distinct advantage in the commercial arena because he could marry technical aspects with finance requirements. He believes professionals often make the mistake of thinking in silos based on the disciplines they studied and the roles they subsequently assume – and this limits the quality of their decision making.

A MOVE TO ENGLAND

Hanré's craving for greater business knowledge led him to apply for an MBA at the University of Oxford's Saïd Business School in 2003. His wife, Karla, whom he married in 2001, accompanied him to London, where she furthered her medical studies.

Sasol's Hanré Rossouw *(Photo: Geoff Brown)*

The hostile exchange rate made light work of depleting the couple's rand-denominated savings, forcing Hanré to get a job as a project manager at De Beers in London. This exposed him to marketing, as his role involved supporting mining site holders setting out to monetise their diamond extracts.

'When you walk out of business school with an MBA, you think you're the king of the world and you expect job offers to be thrown your way. The reality is quite the opposite; I actively had to look for a placement. I realised that even with an MBA, you need to determine what your niche is to help you get a suitable role. I came full circle when I started looking at mining companies for my next gig.'

Hanré applied to big mining houses such as Anglo American and the then BHP Billiton and was busy with intense interviews and psychometric tests when a friend suggested that he speak to the 'crazy people at Xstrata'. At the time, they had a small office above the famous Tiger Tiger night club near Piccadilly Circus where Hanré sat down for a cup of coffee with the CEO, Mick Davis.

After the interview, as he was halfway down Leicester Square on his way to the London Underground, Davis called and offered him a job. That was the beginning of a ten-year rollercoaster ride with the Anglo-Swiss multinational mining company.

'It was an incredible opportunity to be part of the Mergers and Acquisitions team of a group that was building up a portfolio of mining assets. Mick was very empowering; he was the type of leader who encouraged employees to pursue opportunities without bureaucratic red tape that would stifle our entrepreneurial spirit,' Hanré reminisces.

Hanré got to travel to every continent and learnt many things, including the principles of effective capital allocation, how to finance transactions and integrating businesses post acquisition. After listing on the London Stock Exchange in 2002 and making global acquisitions worth approximately US$40 billion, Xstrata grew to be the fifth largest international mining house six years later.

It wasn't always easy. There were some disappointments along the way, like the time when the company had been pursuing an acquisition in Australia that included a six-month due diligence process. Hanré and the team flew from London to Perth to finalise the deal, only to find that

BHP had swooped in at the last minute to outbid them.

Dejected, the team flew back to London. 'To our surprise, Mick took us out for what he called a celebratory dinner where we popped a bottle of one of the finest champagnes. In his view, we needed to fete the fact that we had not overpaid for the business.

'There was an important life lesson in that experience. We are often upset when things do not go our way, not thinking it might be a blessing in disguise. That deal would have turned out to be a really bad investment at the price point we would have needed to get if we'd had to close it.'

Hanré's involvement in these deals went beyond securing the purchase transaction. The skills he acquired at Accenture came in handy, as he and his team had to unlock synergies to ensure that what was promised when the investment case was put together would actually be delivered.

In October 2007, Hanré was appointed Head of Investor Relations. This exposed him to capital markets, as the role required participating in raising capital for projects.

RETURNING TO SOUTH AFRICA

'My wife and I had settled into life in London. In the spring of 2011, we were expecting our second child and we had also just bought a house in Oxford. Mick called me to his office one day to offer me the CFO position at Xstrata Alloys in South Africa. I remember going home that day to find Karla putting up curtains in our new home. I had to tell her we were returning to South Africa.'

Nearly ten years after the couple flew to England with nothing but two suitcases, they returned with a container of stuff and two children. Hanré enjoyed his new job, which also entailed setting up an employee share scheme and optimising the operational finance function and shared services.

In April 2013, Glencore completed the takeover of Xstrata, which led to the departure of both Mick Davis and the group CFO, Trevor Reid. Hanré felt a void had been created by the exit of his two mentors and so he started shopping around for a new job. During the time of evaluating options post the Xstrata journey, Investec approached him to head up resources investment in frontier and emerging markets.

'The post was based in Cape Town, which was attractive, because I had always felt I'd uprooted Karla from her hometown. She had put up with me as I travelled all over the world and this was my chance to bring her back home,' says Hanré, with a proud grin on his face.

Other than scoring brownie points with his wife, the move also gave Hanré an opportunity to see things from the other side of the table. Up until that point, he had been working for mining companies, trying to convince investors to give them money for projects. Now he was working as an investor, assessing the pleas for funding from players in the resources industry.

'The people at Investec are a brilliant bunch. The role taught me about the offset between risk and reward and gave me perspectives on assessing share prices against the true value of companies. I found that investors had a big role in shaping the world, because they have the ability to demand that companies do not merely pay lip service to environmental, social and governance objectives.'

In June 2018, one of the directors at Royal Bafokeng Platinum (RB-Plat) approached Hanré about taking up the group CFO role at the company. Hanré wasn't looking for a new job at the time, but he agreed to have a cup of coffee with the RBPlat CEO, Steve Phiri, with whom he had interacted a few times before.

The discussions with Phiri convinced Hanré to take on yet another new challenge. The company was a medium-size player in the platinum industry, which would give him the opportunity to take part in the creation of something bigger. In addition, RBPlat was the only community-owned company that was listed on the Johannesburg Stock Exchange, which made it attractive for someone like Hanré, who wanted to make a real difference in communities.

Hanré used his mining experience to contribute to the development of the Styldrift mine. 'The business of mining is very tricky, and your success is highly dependent on timing. You need to invest in the development of mining assets at the bottom of the commodity cycle, when prices are low, and ensure that those assets are ready to serve the market by the time the cycle is at the top, when prices are high.'

Executing this plan involved a number of activities, such as concluding a US$145 million streaming arrangement with the mining house

Triple Flag. In July 2020, RBPlat financed a 200-bed field hospital in Rustenburg to support COVID-19 treatment and delivered record profits despite the pandemic. This enabled RBPlat to give decent returns to their shareholders.

'Paying dividends is very important. Many mining companies think of shareholders as the last person who should expect to see returns, but my view is that they should be at the centre of everything we do. The project teams at RBPlat did heroic work in enabling these returns in tough market conditions,' Hanré says.

In July 2021, news broke that Hanré will be taking over as CFO of the petrochemicals group Sasol, with his official joining date set for April 2022 following a lengthy and structured handover period.

'I'm joining Sasol at a time when the world is confronted by climate change and the group has to reimagine its future. Sasol has been going through a difficult time and the balance sheet has been shaken tremendously. A lot has been done to right the ship and my job will be to assist in the continued recovery.'

STRATEGIES FOR SUCCESS

This role at Sasol will require Hanré to draw on previous lessons from putting together successful strategies. From a theoretical point of view, he mentions the need to consider the five forces described by Professor Michael Porter of the Harvard Business School: the threat of new entrants; internal competition; the threat of substitutes; customer bargaining power; and supplier bargaining power.

From a practical perspective, a strategy has to be agile, says Hanré. A formal document helps shape thinking, but management needs to balance risk and reward. It is tempting to be conservative and run a stable company that pays regular dividends to its shareholders. However, for a company to achieve its true potential, it needs to take risks and place bets that could potentially progress it from good to great.

Looking back, there isn't much Hanré would have done differently in his career. He is grateful for the opportunities he had and the lessons he learnt from mentors, one of the biggest being the importance of listening to others. He also believes that you should use the knowledge you acquire to develop other people, which includes training them to take over your job. Being protective of your position and preventing others from succeeding you stifles your own growth, he says.

'It's important to be patient as you move up the corporate ladder,' Hanré continues. 'Always seek to have an element of uncertainty and discomfort, which will nudge you to stretch yourself in what you do. Take note of the learnings that come your way and don't rush; you need to crawl before you can walk, and you need to walk before you can run.'

Hanré advises against engaging in 'corridor politics', where individuals put their interests before those of the organisation. This includes turf wars in which professionals share information selectively because they want to outdo their colleagues. This is 'the cancer that kills organisations', he says.

Management should recognise that people inherently want to succeed. It is unnecessary to control everything they do, for example by monitoring what time they check in and out. This creates distrust, while employees need to feel supported to excel. According to Hanré, a leader should also aim to understand each team member and allow them to fail from time to time, as it is part of the learning process.

Asked what he is reading at the moment, Hanré pulls out a copy of *Crucial Conversations: Tools for Talking when Stakes are High*, a bestselling business read. He is also a keen reader of other genres and his favourite novel is *The Murmur of Bees* by Sofía Segovia. Of the many biographies he has read, he recommends *Fortunes: The Rise and Rise of Afrikaner Tycoons* by Ebbe Dommisse.

Hanré hasn't planned his future beyond the task ahead of him at Sasol. His next move has always been determined by a simple quest: seeking out new challenges and finding solutions to new problems to avoid getting bored.

MARK STIRTON

Daring to be different

— INTERVIEW: APRIL 2021 —

The word 'average' simply is not part of Mark Stirton's vocabulary. He might be a chartered accountant, but he has always had entrepreneurial flair. He believes in the power of technology to make strategy work and is not afraid to think differently.

After completing his three-year articles at PwC in Durban in early 2005, Mark briskly headed for the exit door. He quickly realised auditing was not his dream job and he has never looked back.

He joined Eurotap South Africa, an investment company owned by Doug Lumley in KwaZulu-Natal with various business interests. His time at Eurotap reminds Mark of the third season of the reality TV series *The Apprentice*, where highly educated graduates dubbed 'the booksmarts' teamed up against less academic, business-minded contestants called 'the streetsmarts'.

'I think the move from PwC to Eurotap shifted me from being book smart to street smart,' he says.

Lumley taught him to always be in touch with what happens on the ground in a company, a valuable lesson that, to this day, he shares with his mentees. 'One night, Doug called me and told me to meet him at an injection moulding factory [one of the company's businesses] the next day. He told me to wear shorts, which I found quite strange. When I got there, I found him packing a truck all by himself. Doug explained that he had been looking at supplier invoices and was not convinced we were getting value for money, so he was packing the truck to establish the exact volume of goods each vehicle could carry.'

The experience taught Mark to always 'pack the truck' himself, no matter how high up he was on the corporate ladder. 'There is immense value in taking a walk through the ground level of operations and understanding the business,' he says.

After eight years at Eurotap, Mark was head-hunted to join Aspen Pharmacare, the largest producer of generic medicines in Africa, as commercial manager for the group. He was excited at the prospect of working with the founder, Stephen Saad, who, according to Mark, is 'one of the best entrepreneurs Durban has ever produced'.

He was approached by Mr Price less than a year later. Although he enjoyed his time at Aspen, the idea of working in the fashion industry appealed to him 'because of the kind of creativity that is required to excel in that space'.

Clothing retailer Mr Price was founded in 1985 and has 1 417 stores across the African continent. The group brands include Mr Price, Mr Price Home, Mr Price Sport, Miladys, Mr Price Money, Sheet Street and, most recently, also Yuppiechef and Power Fashion. The company is one of the Top 40 companies on the Johannesburg Stock Exchange .

Mark was appointed as group financial manager for special projects in June 2014 and later moved on to the position of corporate finance director, which involved integrating group initiatives into divisional structures and driving enhancements across the various businesses. His promotion to CFO in January 2019, at the age of 38, was a definite career highlight.

'I was humbled to be given this role in a company that has an amazing track record and with great people before me having steered the business to financial health. I feel encouraged that they've entrusted me with navigating the ship at a relatively young age. I think having developed my own style for going about things will help us solve problems quicker.'

Mr Price's Mark Stirton *(Photo: Dalisu Ngobese)*

GROWTH THROUGH ACQUISITIONS

Since Mark's appointment, the group has undertaken two significant acquisitions. In the first, Yuppiechef, a predominantly online retailer of upmarket kitchen products, was bought in a deal worth close to half a billion rand in March 2021.

That same month, the Competition Commission also approved their intended acquisition of Power Fashion, a clothing retailer with 170 stores focused on the low- to middle-income market.

These acquisitions signify the growth ambitions of the two Marks at the heart of Mr Price's corporate suite – Stirton as CFO and Mark Blair, his predecessor and now CEO. It has also drawn positive media reaction. Financial journalist Sasha Planting writes that after Mr Price could not put a foot wrong in the decade leading up to the mid-2000s, it seemed to have lost its sparkle as growth and the share price slowed. However, 'a revised strategy (of acquisitions) appears to be infusing new energy into the group'.

I ask Mark what makes a successful strategy.

'You need to have a vision of what could be and what should be. You then link that vision with a purpose that transcends short-term return. You need to aim to capture the hearts and minds of people, and combine that with the right business model. Strategy is the plan you pursue to actualise the vision.'

The topic of strategy reminds Mark of the book *Blue Ocean Shift: Beyond Competing*, a *New York Times* bestseller. 'I learnt a lot from the book, including how to create uncontested market spaces. Michael Porter [a renowned business strategist] says that you either win on cost or win on differentiation, but the authors of *Blue Ocean Shift* talk about value innovation. They write about creating value that is so significant that you need not compete on cost or differentiation alone.'

Mark explains that this centres around creating great products without having to price them cheaply. 'That is the "blue ocean", where customers actually find *you*, rather than you having to seek them out through the "red ocean", where it is a race to the bottom with companies undercutting each other on price.'

He also believes in using technology to implement a strategy. With the increased use of smart devices on the continent – 475 million people are projected to be mobile internet users by 2025 – Mark believes a digital revolution is on its way.

'For commercial purposes, communicating and transacting through mobile apps will become the norm, particularly in a post-COVID environment, where there is likely to be behavioural change. Organisations that are digitally ready will have a significant advantage over those that are not,' he projects.

The strength of Yuppiechef's e-commerce platform was therefore a key consideration when Mr Price looked at acquiring the company.

'You can be average in repetitive transactional activities because those are not the things that you win on,' says Mark. 'But you must be brilliant at the activities that are pivotal to success, which include strategic thinking and execution.'

USING TECHNOLOGY TO TRANSFORM A BUSINESS

Mark believes technological innovation should also be used to improve efficiencies in a company. When he arrived at Mr Price, the finance function's reporting was all done in spreadsheets.

'A lot of transformation has happened – and is still happening – to get our finance function to operate on an integrated and seamless basis. I cringed seeing the team get through monthly and annual reporting in such a manual way, which was also very time and energy consuming.'

Mark's passion for digital transformation has led him to pursue an executive MBA, with a focus on global digital business.

'I'm a crusader for deploying technology, because systems can propel you to do more strategic and catalytic work. The traditional CFO gets boxed in the stewardship mindset to maintain the business and work for the system. As a result, 85% of your time is spent working to *report* the numbers, while 15% of your time is left to *understand* the numbers.'

Mark is trying to flip this by getting finance leaders in the group to spend more than two-thirds of their time on transformation and forward-thinking processes, to become what he calls 'strategic catalysts'.

'The finance leader should be such a thinker that when the MD or commercial leader comes with an idea, the CFO is ready to assist in making it work. The CFO should be ready to put meat on the bone and catalyse corporate action.'

Besides his formal qualifications and accreditation – chartered accountant, Fellow of the Chartered Institute of Management Accountants, MBA – Mark spends a lot of time reading on business and leadership.

'Reading about how the best people out there are going about their business enables me to benchmark our approach to our global peers. South Africa does a lot of things well, but I think we're still three or four years behind in terms of thinking about things like robotics in the workplace. So I'm improving my skill set to bring a different lens to problem solving and reframing how finance is conceived and perceived.'

An example of the changes Mark is putting in place at Mr Price relates to the external audit process. In the tender for a new external auditor, Mark will be looking for an auditing company that does things differently. 'I view the auditor as a partner to help me identify and mitigate risk. So rather than coming in at year-end to audit our numbers, I plan on having them plugged into our system and accessing live data throughout the year.'

In Mark's view, this will not only enable the auditor to identify risks but will also result in cost savings from having fewer staff members involved in the audit. In addition, he has created what they call the 'Advanced' business unit in the group to focus on developing data-driven business insights.

'We're creating an insight-driven business, led by people but supported by artificial intelligence. We're constructing an enterprise data factory that will give us information to structure better decisions in real time. Using data and technology is the way of the future.'

Does he have any concerns that an emphasis on technological interventions will lead to job losses?

Mark replies with a quote from Henry Ford: "If I had asked people what they wanted, they would have said faster horses." 'The horse industry was concerned that the invention of the car would render people like blacksmiths redundant, yet it resulted in plenty more manufacturing and related jobs. Innovation will often lead to the birth of new job opportunities.'

DEALING WITH CRISES

Mr Price lost R2 billion in April 2020 when COVID-19 hit, which was almost 50 per cent of the cash reserves of the company. However, Mr Price is a brand that South Africans love, and despite the economic uncertainty, people still wanted to look and feel good, Mark says.

'We've been able to provide affordable value in that regard, which has been reflected in the market share gains we've seen during the pandemic ... We truly believe that we're the people's champion for fashion value.'

The Mr Price team refer to themselves as 'ordinary people doing extraordinary things'. And they put their money where their mouth was during the pandemic, guaranteeing employee salaries during the hard lockdown, despite revenue loss.

'Many companies have these wonderful value statements on their walls, but when it comes down to it, do they live those values when it could cost them financially? At Mr Price, I believe we've proven that we can. For instance, we dealt with our suppliers, like the many landlords who house our stores, differently by approaching them quite early to discuss arrangements that were mutually beneficial.'

The key thing in crisis is the speed and manner of communication, Mark believes. 'When people don't know what is going on, they become paralysed. We approached the crisis by making quick decisions and communicating them clearly. In a flat structure like ours, divisional leaders know the parameters within which they can act, without having to wait for approval from above.'

Mr Price has a strong balance sheet, which has been managed well over the years, and this was a critical factor for managing the storm successfully. Many similar businesses have a lot of debt, says Mark, which results in pressure on decision-making and, in turn, cause a compromise on the values that a company sets out.

'Crisis can lead to a change in people's behaviour, which can erode partnerships. A crisis is a time for leadership to step up and prove that the company is really centred on people. Our viewpoint was to try and save jobs, as South Africa can ill afford to have more people unemployed. As a board of directors, we took salary cuts for a six-month period to help preserve cash.'

LESSONS FOR YOUNG PROFESSIONALS

Mark believes that having a growth mindset is essential to ensuring relevance and is fuelled by being a lifelong learner. 'Most of us don't seek to learn new things after we finish school or university and we become closed to change at some level. When you don't actively seek knowledge every day, you become inflexible. This turns into a lack of change in ourselves and our organisations.'

If he were to give advice to his 25-year-old self, Mark says he would emphasise the need to embrace technology early on.

'If I had looked to technology earlier, I would have been able to let technology do monotonous, repetitive tasks and have more time to spend thinking rather than doing,' he reflects. 'I don't think our school curriculum prepares our children for what the world will look like in the future. For this reason, my wife and I are exploring enrolling our three kids in computer-coding classes – not necessarily to become programmers but to understand what future artists will use and its endless possibilities for life and business.'

Another piece of advice to his younger self is to take people with you on a transformation journey from early on. Most companies in South Africa are either digitally antiquated or recent digital converts, he says. 'Businesses like Tesla and Google are digitally native, which makes them highly flexible and adaptable and so they can perform and transform simultaneously. I would therefore encourage my younger self to get the appropriate psychology skills to manage change better.'

While there are a few things he would have wanted to know at a younger age, Mark is confident in his strategic outlook and management style.

'I believe in the concept of future-back thinking. Essentially, you envision the future you want, and then develop the initiatives needed to make it happen. I then adopt a concept I learnt from the founder of the Ritz-Carlton Hotels, who regularly reminds employees that they've been "chosen" for their roles. This inspires them to put their hearts into what they do, because they know that they've been carefully selected to do what others cannot, to realise the future.'

By thinking out of the box and daring to be different, this 'strategic catalyst' continues to lead by example.

MIKE DAVIS

Artist of the balance sheet

— INTERVIEW: OCTOBER 2020 —

Mike Davis's career in banking started over two decades ago when he joined NBS (previously the Natal Building Society) in 1998. His appointment as CFO of the Nedbank group from 1 October 2020 means he has basically been with the bank for more than 20 years, seeing that Nedbank effectively incorporated NBS through a series of mergers.

He was previously the executive responsible for balance sheet management, and has been a member of the group's executive committee since January 2015. I spoke to him about a month after he started in his new role.

Mike explains that he entered accounting on his father's advice. 'My father wasn't a CA [chartered accountant], but having been in business he thought highly of the profession and encouraged my brother and me to go that route. He told us we would study to become CAs; after that we could do whatever we wanted.'

Mike completed his BCom degree and a higher diploma in accountancy at the (former) University of Natal and then joined Deloitte in 1994 for his three-year articles. That was followed by a stint in Deloitte's New York office on secondment in early 1998.

Mike returned to Deloitte in Durban after his secondment and was offered a position at the firm. But he declined it, as he had already made up his mind to pursue a career in banking, having been deployed to the NBS audit from his first year at Deloitte.

'Initially when I joined in 1998, I worked in the group risk ambit, which fell under the auspices of the group credit function,' Mike recalls. 'I then moved across to the asset and liability management area, also within Group Risk. This subsequently evolved into a fully fledged balance sheet management function, which effectively straddles group risk, finance and treasury functions and handles multiple accounting and regulatory responsibilities.'

This part of the business has been central to Mike's role and, given the number of mergers Nedbank has been involved in, it has been quite exciting for him to integrate this discipline across merged entities.

Not many professionals stay at one company as long as Mike has. He explains that the mergers were engaging: NBS merged with Boland Bank, then NBS Boland merged with BoE and later all three were absorbed into Nedbank. These mergers consumed the better part of six years, and it takes a while for a company to return from an inward to an outward focus after every merger. And with every merger there are new processes to be learnt and platforms to be integrated, together with the inevitable competition for positions.

'In 2003, following the last merger with Nedbank, I moved to Johannesburg, where my role was expanded into balance sheet management. This included capital management as well as several risk-adjusted performance measurement processes. The dynamic nature of my role has kept me thoroughly engaged over the years.'

Not many of us are familiar with the concept of balance sheet management in banking. But it helps to think about it in terms of a bank having many businesses. For most banks, the foremost activities are lending money and taking deposits. Lending money represents assets, while deposits represent liabilities. Liabilities such as fixed deposits are relatively short in tenor and are raised at a fixed interest rate, whereas assets such as home loans have a longer tenor and are typically priced at a variable interest rate. The divergence in tenor and rate type presents liquidity and interest rate risks or mismatches, which require active management.

Capital risk also comes into play, because a bank is required to raise

Nedbank's Mike Davis *(Photo: Neil Kirby)*

a portion of its funds as capital to absorb unexpected losses. As a result, balance sheet management also entails making decisions about how much and what tier of capital a bank should hold.

'I've been involved with managing those risks, and this culminated in my appointment to the role of group executive for balance sheet management in 2015,' Mike says. 'Initially I reported directly to the COO [chief operating officer] and for the last two years to my predecessor, Raisibe Morathi. Given the nature of my previous role, I was well positioned for the role of CFO.'

BALANCING ACT

Mike has been a firm proponent of developing a strong risk culture and risk discipline within the group, and being appointed CFO of one of Africa's largest banks in the middle of a pandemic is a challenging prospect.

'I don't see it as necessarily a good or a bad thing,' he reflects. 'I see it simply as an opportunity. The results belong to us as an executive team and ultimately the board. If the results improve from here, credit goes to the team for executing the strategy appropriately.'

'We've also been investing heavily in our client experiences through technology. Since 2014, we've been putting the foundational technology in place so that our clients can have the same pleasant experience whether they engage with the bank through a branch, their phone or a laptop.'

'Through balance sheet management, we've contributed to driving competitive client experience through pricing, product, capital deployment and risk-adjusted processes.'

Mike also serves as the joint chairman of the group's modernisation workstream, which manages the refactoring of the back-end technology framework needed for delivering a simplified front-end client experience.

'I'm proud to have contributed to building the team that we have under the balance sheet management discipline. It's a well-diversified, competent team of top talent working in an exciting environment. It's a pleasure to come to work every day. When you spend so much time together, it's important that you enjoy the company of the people you work with.'

Mike says he feels privileged to have a team of top talent, which can be managed in a flat structure.

'The team know that we have an open-door policy. If anyone has an issue, they're always welcome to speak to me directly. I'm also happy to roll up my sleeves and get stuck into the detail; in fact, I really enjoy the detail of what we do. It makes me confident about the overall results. I like to surround myself with people who are good on a technical level and who have a strong work ethic. If you can build that type of resource pool, being efficient and effective as a team becomes so much easier.'

Like any other institution, Nedbank has had both successful and difficult years. The group is based largely in South Africa, with a limited international franchise and a growing footprint in the rest of Africa.

'We have extremely good people and a great culture, and we're driving a common purpose. This has helped us deal with various challenges, including the COVID-19 pandemic.'

Bank shares are directly correlated to the macroeconomic environment. And of course low interest rates adversely impact on bank margins. In a risk-off environment, where the long end of the yield curve steepens – as it did as a result of COVID-19 – bank stock prices fall as margins squeeze and prices are discounted off higher, risk-free rates. In effect this is a double whammy for share valuations. During the pandemic Nedbank's management pivoted their strategy to resilience before shifting to reimagining the future.

PLANNING AHEAD

In taking up his new role, Mike immediately put together a structured plan on what he wanted to achieve over the short, medium and long term, including any developmental areas identified during his interview process. He began engaging with members of the board, the executive committee and his finance team soon after his appointment to understand their expectations, and also had to focus on some big deliverables straightaway, such as the third quarter forecast, the bank's three-year planning process, investor road shows and the year-end reporting.

All these plans were made against the backdrop of the complexities arising from a macroeconomic environment that was reeling from the effects of COVID-19.

'One of my primary goals is to leave a legacy of having added value from a financial, strategic, risk and audit perspective. This means ensuring that our financial and risk reporting is free of material issues and provides value-adding insights. I also look forward to having an active role in managing and driving the strategy of the organisation. This will involve working closely with Mike Brown, our CE [chief executive] and the board in executing our three-year business plans.'

The CFOs of the bank's various businesses report to their respective executive management clusters, and have a dotted line to Mike as the group's CFO. He plans on building stronger relationships across that finance horizontal to create efficiencies and leverage their combined finance skills.

'I will also continue to be involved in improving optimisation, bringing down our costs, driving top-line revenue growth and developing our technology to deliver better client experiences. And putting on my previous hat, I'll keep on driving the shape of our balance sheet, leveraging it to grow our transactional banking franchise.'

In light of his international work experience, I was curious as to whether Mike has ever considered emigrating.

'I think, like most professionals, you wonder at some point whether the grass is greener abroad,' he admits. 'Along the way, many of my colleagues have moved to places like Australia and the United Kingdom. For most, the concern is what the future will hold for South Africa.

'I've been very fortunate. Being part of this organisation has presented me with many opportunities, including most recently my appointment to the CFO role. I enjoy working for Nedbank and I cherish the people I work with. I embrace our culture and I appreciate what we're trying to achieve collectively.'

MEROONISHA KERBER

The nice girl in the corner office

— INTERVIEW: APRIL 2021 —

As financial director of Impala Platinum – which is one of the 40 biggest companies on the Johannesburg Stock Exchange employing over 50 000 people and generating R70 billion in revenue a year – Meroonisha Kerber holds one of the most senior roles in corporate South Africa. Despite the pre-eminence of her position, she exudes humility and a sense of calm.

The *New York Times* bestseller *Nice Girls Don't Get the Corner Office* by Lois P Frankel explores how women get overlooked for promotion because of certain behavioural traits that result in their being viewed as not worthy of top positions. As a Muslim woman of colour, Meroonisha has had to deal with several of these 'nice girl' challenges on her way to the corner office.

She has been called out for working through lunch instead of socialising with colleagues and was once criticised for not fraternising in the bar on Friday evenings. (Fridays are a day of worship in Islam and it is against her religious beliefs to consume alcohol.) This 'unsocial' behaviour was listed as an aspect for career development, something she was unwilling to accept. Her ascension to the role of CFO has proven that bending to generally accepted norms need not be the way to get ahead.

'Women are judged by a different yardstick from men,' she says. 'Some things that are seen as weaknesses are actually strengths. For example, we are in tune with our emotions, which makes us more empathetic managers and we often develop more profound relationships with our teams and colleagues. I think my having stayed in touch with many of my ex-colleagues is testament to that. We don't need to change; we should stay true to ourselves.'

Meroonisha, who always pauses before responding to a question, says she thinks it is unnecessary for women to feel that they need to be as forceful as men in the male-dominated world of finance. Her advice to female managers is to lead their teams in a way that is authentic to them, instead of trying to emulate their male counterparts' approach.

But at the same time she advises women to be more assertive about their rights. 'If I had a time machine and could go back, I would not be as accepting as I was about the differences I've seen between men's and women's promotion and remuneration,' she says.

RISING TO THE TOP

Meroonisha is a humble CFO, with a humble background. She grew up in a modest family; her parents could not afford to pay for her Bachelor of Commerce degree and postgraduate studies at Rhodes University in Grahamstown. Her younger brother took out a student loan to bolster her partial bursaries and she had to outperform her classmates to scoop up scholarships that would settle the balance of her fees.

She graduated from Rhodes in 1994 and joined Deloitte in East London for articles a year later. She was appointed an audit manager in the mining division in 1997, a position she held until 2005 when she joined Anglo American Platinum (Amplats), which was one of her clients. She had various roles at Amplats, including being the manager responsible for consolidation and group accounting, technical accounting and financial accounting.

One of her career highlights was being part of establishing the Amplats Kotula Trust in June 2008, which is a broad-based employee share ownership scheme in which over 46 000 employees have participated. She also participated in Amplats's broad-based economic

Impala Platinum's Meroonisha Kerber *(Photo: Patrick Furter)*

empowerment initiative, Alchemy, which was created in 2011. This multibillion rand empowerment transaction gave South African host communities an opportunity to own shares in the world's largest primary platinum producer.

In 2016, she left Anglo American to take up the position of senior vice-president at AngloGold Ashanti (AGA). Her move to AGA was inspired by two considerations. First, she would be working in a company dealing in a different commodity; second, she would get exposure to a company that was regulated by the United States Securities and Exchange Commission.

At AGA, Meroonisha worked closely with then CEO Srinivasan (Venkat) Venkatakrishnan and then CFO Christine Ramon. She was learning much from these two inspiring colleagues and had no plans of leaving the company. But then, in August 2018, she was head-hunted for the position of CFO at Impala Platinum, a challenging opportunity in an industry that she was passionate about.

'When I look back, I probably took a bit longer than most CFOs to be appointed to the role. I think this is because it was not my ambition to become one from the start. When I left auditing, I was just looking to find a space where I could enjoy what I did, where the work would be challenging and where I could feel that I was making a positive contribution,' she says.

Meroonisha accepted the Implats offer because she felt that she had been supporting CFOs all along and was now ready to become a decision-maker. Having honed her technical skills in the platinum business for over a decade, she also had a solid experience base to lead a finance team in that space.

DEALING WITH CRISIS AT IMPLATS

When Meroonisha joined Implats, a decade of depressed platinum prices had forced the company to announce retrenchment plans, in which she had to play a central part as financial director. She also found out that she was pregnant soon after starting at Implats, which meant that she would have to go on maternity leave just a few months after assuming office.

The surprise baby shower her colleagues threw for her was one of her happiest workplace moments. CEO Nico Muller and the rest of the board of directors were also very supportive during the time she was away. Platinum prices fortunately also rebounded, which improved the company's profitability and financial position and allowed them to look at other operational improvements rather than retrenching employees. Crisis averted.

Meroonisha projects the image of someone who always has things under control. When it comes to dealing with crises, she believes in prevention rather than cure. 'I prefer to avert the point of crisis by putting the right processes and controls in place,' she says. 'By regular, transparent engagement, people feel comfortable to escalate issues, which then gives us ample time to respond. Open communication gives us the kind of space where we can engage and debate the pros and cons of possible options and determine the best course of action.'

The COVID-19 pandemic is an example of a recent crisis she had to deal with. Mining was one of the sectors that were allowed to operate during the hard lockdown in April and May 2020, albeit at a reduced level of production. Whereas commodity prices were high, the company faced several challenges, such as implementing safety protocols at their mines and the shortage of flights to transport product. Stagnating sales created a liquidity gap, because fixed obligations such as salaries and suppliers still had to be paid.

This was a balancing act for the executive management team. 'We had to take some difficult decisions, including asking our employees to take both paid and unpaid leave,' she recalls. 'This was in the early stages when we didn't have a good understanding of the impact of the pandemic and whether we would be allowed to operate fully. We're grateful that in the end we were and that metal prices were favourable, which allowed us to give returns to our shareholders, who had been waiting for a long time for dividends. We also managed to pay our suppliers on time, which is important because a lot of them depend on us for their livelihood.'

Lessons learnt from the pandemic include the importance of having capital discipline. Mining companies often have costly capital projects with long lead times, financed by a product that is cyclical in nature.

The coronavirus crisis reaffirmed the need to be risk averse in project selection and execution.

The company's resilience to the pandemic was supported by initiatives taken in preceding years, such as successfully converting US-denominated debt to equity and so reducing debt subject to significant interest payments. As a result, in the first year Meroonisha was at the helm of finances, the group ended with net cash of R1.1 billion compared with debt of R5.3 billion the previous year.

The following year the company's net cash position improved even further – to R5.7 billion – and the company hit record headline earnings (R16 billion) despite dealing with the pandemic. The improved financial position enabled the company to complete the acquisition of North American Palladium in Canada. One of the benefits of the deal was the diversification of the group's presence outside of South Africa and Zimbabwe, where regulatory challenges and electricity constraints affect operations.

FINDING A SOUNDING BOARD

Effective communication is essential for a successful strategy, says Meroonisha. 'You need to be open to listen to other people's views. You also need to make sure that you're well informed about the subject matter by researching the issue. That includes talking to different people. When you do so, be selective in who you seek advice from; focus on subject matter experts.'

Meroonisha also advises professionals to keep a list of a few people other than subject experts who they trust implicitly to speak to about work situations confidentially. She has a few colleagues she calls upon in this regard and she also schedules regular sessions with an executive coach. These people are valuable sounding boards.

She also regards communication as a key requirement for building effective teams, whether people are introverts or extroverts. It is important to articulate your ideas and to be honest about areas you may be struggling with, so that colleagues will know how to support you. Meroonisha finds that employees who are willing to take advice and constructive feedback on board climb the corporate ladder faster because they learn from their leaders and peers.

She thinks of herself as a good listener, never missing a beat when I chime in with a joke during our interview. Her hearty laughter shows she doesn't take herself too seriously.

She also admires employees who take advantage of opportunities in the workplace. 'Good employees are eager to be involved in new projects and think of innovative ways to do things,' she says. 'They work hard and ensure that they deliver. Consistency is key; it shows they can be relied upon. They also treat their colleagues with respect, regardless of position.'

According to her, the ideal employee does not simply present a problem, but comes with possible solutions. This indicates that they have thought through the problem. 'The proposed solution may not be the one we go with in the end, but at least it gives us a starting point for exploring different ways to resolve the issue.'

Having good technical knowledge equips a professional to do their work meaningfully and Meroonisha therefore encourages employees to dedicate time to continued learning.

MANAGING FOR CHANGE

Continued learning is something Meroonisha practises herself too, focusing particularly on change management.

'When you start in a new position, there are usually quite a few things that you want to change,' she says. 'When making those changes, you have to be cognisant of the people in the organisation and the rate at which they can handle change. You need strong direct reports to support you in this quest. It's a difficult balance, because on the one hand you have a board that expects results and on the other hand you need to ease your team into the transformation you're trying to effect.'

To this end you need to understand what you are trying to achieve and why things were done a certain way in the past and identify the people who can help you bring about change. According to Meroonisha ensuring that the team understand why a different direction is necessary is an important part of successful change management.

'This approach means change may ultimately take longer to come about, but it's more important to get people's buy-in and to take them with you than to do things hurriedly on your own. In fact, sometimes you may have an idea of how something should be done. But rather than spell it out, it's better to guide your team to come up with a few suggestions themselves, so that they take ownership of decisions.'

Guiding staff is a key feature of Meroonisha's management style. Although she doesn't always agree with everyone, she does her best to ensure people feel that they have been heard. 'I always try to get my team to speak out when they don't agree with me, and they regularly surprise me with things I had not thought of. Considering different viewpoints allows us to find the most robust solution.'

Managing people calls for considering their personal circumstances, says Meroonisha. She recognises that people's lives span different roles. 'You work with a person in their entirety. If you understand their mental and emotional space, you can accommodate them appropriately and hopefully bring out the best in them. This may require some flexibility in what you expect from different team members.'

Staff also need to be suitably equipped to deliver – insufficient or inappropriate resources should not be the reason objectives are not achieved. And despite her caring and humble approach, Meroonisha doesn't shy away from difficult and honest discussions with staff who are underperforming. The 'nice girl' in the corner office has a human touch in everything she does, but she also knows what it takes to get the job done.

ABIGAIL MUELELWA MUKHUBA

The girl who chose the shortest queue

— INTERVIEW: JULY 2021 —

Abigail Mukhuba might have entered the world of finance by chance, but once she got started there was no stopping this woman with the steely resolve. She had set herself the goal to become the finance director of a listed company by the age of 40, which she achieved when she was appointed CFO of African Rainbow Minerals (ARM) in December 2017.

Resolve is often the opposite of a simple stubbornness. This was clear from Abigail's decision not to apply to any university in her matric year at Jeppe High School for Girls in Johannesburg. She had set her heart on going to Rhodes University in Grahamstown, but her mother, Matodzi, refused, not wanting her daughter to be so far away from her. This after Abigail had spent the better part of her childhood with her grandparents in Venda and only joined her teacher mother in Johannesburg five years before.

Consequently, the only option was to register for a correspondence course at the University of South Africa. Abigail initially thought a Bachelor of Arts degree would be a good idea, but after hours in the queue to register for this course, she noticed that the line for a Bachelor of Accounting Science degree was much shorter. And that's how Abigail ended up studying to become a bean-counter.

She soon realised that she was quite good at crunching numbers. She graduated in 1999 and obtained an honours degree in accounting from the Rand Afrikaans University (University of Johannesburg today) the next year. In 2001, she joined KPMG for articles. All the trainees aimed to get into financial services audits, the division thought to be the place to be in the firm. Abigail did not, and this set her on a path that gave her international work experience and a better idea about what she wanted out of her career.

At the German Business Group, she had DaimlerChrysler as a client, and when BMW started their articles programme in 2003, Abigail cancelled her KPMG contract and moved to the carmaker. She made the change because she had realised she did not enjoy the auditing process that much as it did not give her sufficient insight into the real business engines. She was posted to BMW's Munich office in 2006, but started to miss home after a few months … Perhaps her mother was right about being far away after all!

TEARS AND TRIBULATIONS

Seeking to work in a local company, she joined Exxaro in 2007 and entered the mining industry. She stayed there for nine years, a time in which she learnt many important lessons, including about crisis management and perseverance.

There have been a few times in her career when Abigail has been driven to tears. Some were while working as a financial manager for Wim de Klerk, then financial director at Exxaro.

One time, after she had prepared what she thought was the perfect presentation, he proceeded to make several changes – which she did not agree with. When she protested, he kicked her out of his office, declaring that he was not prepared to work with her if she wouldn't listen to instructions.

'I had gone in thinking that I've been doing this for years and a new CFO needs to know how we do things. He quickly put me in my place. I was miserable for weeks, but later realised that this was an important lesson. He was showing me how he wanted things done, and I was either with him or against him. If I was with him, we would go far together.

Sanlam's Abigail Muelelwa Mukhuba *(Photo: Geoff Brown)*

But if I was against him, then he would not waste any time on me.'

Abigail mentions another occasion when De Klerk triggered her tears. Exxaro was in the process of investing in Tronox Holdings, an entity listed on the New York Stock Exchange. The finance team had to work over Christmas to meet a filing deadline and were struggling to balance their figures.

Abigail phoned Wim at 3 am and told him about their predicament. He burst out laughing. She was taken aback by his reaction. For a moment she thought he hadn't quite understood her.

'No, Abigail, I understand exactly what you're saying,' Wim retorted. 'And it's hilarious. What do you expect me to do? Tell the Americans that we have a balance sheet that does not balance? That just doesn't happen. Figure it out!'

And with that he hung up.

Needless to say, it left her even more distraught. She ended up crying in the car for an hour and a half because she did not want to break down in front of her team. All she was looking for was some reassurance from her boss, a kind of pep talk that would help her calm down and motivate her to find a solution.

'It taught me that you're not always going to get people to hold your hand. You must dig deep and be self-driven to find the solutions you need. And that is exactly what happened in that case; we picked ourselves up to make one last, solid effort to reconcile the numbers – and succeeded just in time.'

Despite their parting ways a few years ago, De Klerk is one of Abigail's mentors and her favourite boss of all time. She often reaches out to him, and he is always ready to give her advice (now without the tear-inducing sarcastic laughter).

Abigail has since learnt that some of the things she once considered to be the end of the world pale in comparison to some of the issues she has had to face in more senior positions. For example, unearthing accounting errors that necessitate restatement of the financial statements makes her want to pull her hair out.

'I handle a crisis by writing things down. I take a large A3 piece of paper and draw a decision tree to help me figure out what happened and how to avoid it in future. This process also helps me map out the steps that I need to take going forward. Writing down my options and then coming back an hour later or the next day, looking at them with a fresh mind, really helps me make the right calls.'

Working in the mining industry for many years has also helped her realise her strengths as a woman. Abigail believes women should own their femininity and embrace their uniqueness, rather than trying to fit into a predominantly male environment. For instance, at Exxaro, she made a conscious decision to wear dresses to meetings after noticing that men would forget that there was a lady in the room.

'I would also end up forgetting that I am a lady. At some point, I used to use as many swear words as the men, which was completely wrong. You need to show up as a lady and share your perspectives as a lady, rather than getting trapped in group think. A different angle helps a team make better decisions.'

When Riaan Koppeschaar was appointed CFO of Exxaro in 2015, Abigail realised that she was unlikely to realise her dream of becoming the CFO of a listed company by the age of 40 if she stayed on. So, when the opportunity to join ARM came in 2016, she did not hesitate to make the move.

Whereas Exxaro was predominantly a coal mining business, ARM had investments in various resources, which promised to broaden Abigail's experience. She was appointed as the financial director of ARM a year later, after her predecessor, Mike Arnold, retired.

'Being the financial director of a listed entity is different from something like being head of financial reporting,' says Abigail. 'The type of work I was required to do was at a significantly higher level, as was the level of accountability. That said, the move from Exxaro to ARM was fairly seamless, because I was still in mining. The lingo we used was pretty much the same and I was still part of the same network of mining professionals.'

SANLAM AND LIFE AT THE TOP

Moving to Sanlam meant changing to a completely different industry. For Abigail it was a 'crazy transition'.

'At the time I applied for the position, a Sanlam ad referenced a prediction that the first person to live to 200 years old had already been born. If indeed we were destined to live longer, I figured I shouldn't be too concerned by the fact that moving to a new industry was like starting from scratch. I had in any case come full circle, joining the financial services sector all the trainees at KPMG had coveted so many years before.'

Abigail does not shy away from a challenge. She is motivated by the idea of taking on an unfamiliar brief, knowing that although she will undoubtedly make mistakes, she will learn from them. However, the challenge has proven twice as hard as she had imagined.

'The COVID-19 pandemic has made my transition difficult, not only because of the impact on financial performance but also because of not being able to engage with my team physically. It's not easy to figure out who's who in the zoo and develop relationships on virtual platforms.'

Abigail laments the fact that her diary is filled with meetings she would not be required to attend if she was not working remotely. 'They're back to back! I've asked my PA to make my meetings a maximum of 45 minutes to give me a break in between. My nanny told me at one stage I had not been downstairs in three days! I miss sitting in traffic listening to the radio. We did not realise it before, but the commute gave us a breather away from the rigours of office work.'

However, her new job has not been a total den of despondency. There are some similarities with mining, including the long-term nature of Sanlam's investment rationale. And she has since managed to meet the team face to face on several occasions after making a deliberate effort to go into the Johannesburg office and travel to head office in Cape Town. Her team now has a real person to associate with her name and can tell when she is making a joke in a virtual call.

'I love the people who work at Sanlam. They are so helpful and respectful. They remind me of the culture we had at Jeppe Girls, where we were groomed to stop, greet and help our elders in the passages.'

Now that she is part of the executive suite of a Top 40 listed company, Abigail has also come to see things from the other side of the corporate seniority divide. 'Before becoming a director, I didn't realise how lonely it can get at the top of the pyramid. At lower levels, we don't recognise that our seniors are no different from us. They also have good days and bad days; they have their jokes and their serious moments. You should therefore not shy away from engaging them.'

ON ADVICE AND STRATEGY

If Abigail had a time machine that could catapult her back to the start of her career, she would do a lot more travelling. She advises younger professionals to seize any opportunity to see the world and experience different cultures.

Asked about advice for getting ahead, she says you have to actually show up. 'I notice a lot of people just sitting back and hoping somebody will notice them. This is especially true of African professionals. The corporate environment is brutal, and you need to stick your head out and show a desire to be involved. Don't feel like you're asking too many questions; being inquisitive is necessary to improve your knowledge and progress.'

Having recently given birth to her first child, she also has a greater appreciation for working mothers than she did previously. 'Until you have a child yourself, you don't really know how demanding the role can be. I never thought the day would come that I could sit and do nothing while the baby sleeps, simply because I am just too tired. I now have a different appreciation for working parents and their choices of when and how they dedicate time to their children every day.'

On the question of strategy, Abigail believes flexibility is key. In the ever-changing world we're living in, companies should have a long-term vision of what they want to achieve. But they need agility to adjust to what is happening around them.

'A company also needs to appreciate its environment. South African companies struggle when they go into the rest of Africa, because they think of South Africa as being outside of Africa rather than part of the continent. There are similarities between South Africa and other African countries; however, each country has its own, unique circumstances, which need to be acknowledged in the strategy.'

Abigail herself is not afraid to ask for advice. Besides turning to Wim de Klerk, she keeps in touch with former colleagues Mike Arnold and Riaan Koppeschaar to ask their advice about issues they would have dealt with in the past. She also encourages accountability: when things go wrong, she gathers the team and they do a debrief to identify the 'who', the 'what' and the 'why'.

'These are teachable moments, because we all make mistakes that we can learn from. What is important is discussing how we can ensure they do not happen again. Perhaps something was amiss and needs to be provided to avoid the same scenario.'

Through her various roles, Abigail has learnt to be process driven, thinking strategically and critically. Choosing the shortest queue may have worked when she initially got into accounting, but for everything else well-considered decisions have proven to be the best option.

MOHAMMED ABDOOL-SAMAD

Building world-class finance functions

— INTERVIEW: NOVEMBER 2020 —

'A truly decent human being' is how Gavin Dalgleish, current CEO of Illovo Sugar and former colleague, describes Mohammed Abdool-Samad.

'We had a really great relationship,' he says about the time spent working together. 'He was superb to work with. We developed a common understanding of the business and I learnt a lot from him. We had many memorable moments,' Gavin reflects.

One of the most memorable moments was a flight from Zambia to South Africa aboard a small company aircraft. There were only three passengers: he, Mohammed and Ian Parrot, a regional director of the sugar company.

'Mohammed is a devout Muslim and had on a number of occasions taught us about the different facets of his faith, including why he didn't consume alcohol. Ian and I goaded him to have a stiff drink on the flight. We told him that Allah couldn't see him that high up in the sky.'

Mohammed was not buying it and warned that the contravention could lead to some flight trouble.

'He joked that if the plane went down, there was no way his ashes would be confused for mine given my rather large physique. But there was the possibility of Ian's and his body being mixed up, and he could only imagine how upset his father would be to receive the ashes of some

Afrikaans guy who loves to drink instead of his,' Gavin laughs. 'I love the fact that he doesn't take himself so seriously.'

Eerily, one of the engines of the aircraft stopped working, which led to a few nervous moments given the earlier conversation. Fortunately, they landed safely.

FIRST STOP: DELOITTE

Mohammed did not have a privileged upbringing His father worked as an upholsterer in a furniture factory, and his mother was a housewife. He was the middle of three siblings and the first to go to university, courtesy of financial support from the Chartered Accountants' Eden Trust. At university, Mohammed did not have the luxury of 'extracurricular' university life; he had to work part time in the evening as an action cricket umpire to make some money for his upkeep.

'The trust attracted funding from listed companies and my bursary was supported by contributions from the then Barlow Rand,' Mohammed recalls. 'I spent my vacations working at Albany Bakeries, which was a subsidiary of Barlow Rand. I did all manner of things, from cashing in drivers who came back from deliveries to wage payouts and margin analysis. It was great experience.'

During Mohammed's final year of accounting studies at the University of Natal (today the University of KwaZulu-Natal), he was accepted by several of the then Big Five accounting firms for his articles. He chose to join Deloitte because he was of the view that they had a good brand and reputation.

It was 1993 and Mohammed was earning R1 700 per month, which was not a lot of money. He had to live at home and borrow his father's car to get to clients. The travel claims for out-of-town audits supplemented his income.

'The one thing I was sure of was that I didn't want to become an auditor. After qualifying as a CA in 1996, I stayed on at the firm in Durban as a manager and was later involved in building up the Internal Audit and Corporate Governance Practice of Deloitte KwaZulu-Natal (KZN). Companies were still implementing the first King Report on Corporate Governance and I enlisted a number of them as clients to help with that.'

Massmart's Mohammed Abdool-Samad *(Photo: Massmart)*

In the days before functional specialisation, Mohammed was also involved in external and internal audits, forensic work and due diligence for mergers and acquisitions. He also took part in writing and delivering training for disadvantaged universities across South Africa as part of a project sponsored by the United States Agency for International Development.

'In 1998, I landed a contract with Murray & Roberts to do business reviews across all their container and alloy wheel manufacturing facilities across the world. This led to lengthy stints in Europe and Canada.'

While still at Deloitte, he was elected chairman of the local branch of the Institute of Internal Auditors and also qualified as a certified internal auditor. 'There was great versatility in my career at the firm post articles, as I'd been involved in various projects across several industries,' he recalls

Mohammed was not content just to handle a few large audits, which was the simple path to partnership. Instead, he actively set out to expand his business network and try new and sometimes much more complicated things. These were important experiences and development opportunities, which gave him a good grounding for the challenges later on in his career.

'There was no Google in those days. When faced with the unfamiliar, you literally had to sit down and read a book to learn. I would often put my hand up for an assignment I had no clue about, and then go and read or learn from others about how to make it work. I think I was quite a sponge, soaking up knowledge and implementing new things. I wasn't afraid to make mistakes and learn from them.'

Mohammed is passionate about mentoring young professionals and observes that many want to move through the ranks too quickly.

'They're just too eager to get to the top, without the important lateral moves and the rich experiences you get there. You hear them ask, "When am I going to be CFO?" and I counsel them on the importance of soaking up experience, learning and making mistakes. I believe you need the scars from being in the trenches to prove you're ready. I recall being thrown out of a target company's premises during an M&A [merger and acquisition] transaction, defending legal action, bruising board meetings and having the pleasure of meeting heads of state later in my career.

Those are the kinds of things that you need to go through to become battle-hardened for senior roles.'

Mohammed does, however, admit that today's professionals have an advantage when it comes to access to information.

'A 25-year-old today knows much more than I did when I was that age. But I think what happens with their development is that their IQ and EQ don't develop at the same pace. As a result, they have all this knowledge, but often struggle with conflict, influencing, and stepping up as a leader during a crisis. These skills are developed over time. Very few are born with these skills.'

AT ANGLO AMERICAN

Deloitte in London won a contract to help Anglo American with implementing a risk management framework. Mohammed was seconded as part of the South African team called in to help with the assignment after convincing the responsible partner that he would add value to project.

'I was stationed at the Anglo American offices in Main Street, Johannesburg, for eight months. Anglo was the most iconic listed company in South Africa at the time, with the largest market capitalisation on the JSE [Johannesburg Stock Exchange]; everybody wanted to work there. So when I received an offer from Anglo after eight months on contract, I was at a crossroads, given that I was a year or two away from making partnership. I eventually decided to cross over into the corporate world.'

The year 2001 was a landmark year in Mohammed's life. He moved to Johannesburg to join Anglo American, he spent all his money on a pilgrimage to Mecca and his wife, Tasneem, had just given birth to their first child.

'When I joined Anglo, I headed up the risk management team and it was an amazing three years for me. I implemented risk management frameworks, not only in South Africa but also in other markets, including Colombia, Chile, Zambia, Russia and Ireland. I was also part of the King Committee that drafted the second report on corporate governance, specifically the risk management chapter.'

Mohammed realised that he was not keen on immersing himself

in the risk and audit function, so he decided to work towards becoming a CFO. He joined Anglo Coal South Africa as a senior financial manager and was responsible for both financial and management reporting. He had to brush up on his knowledge about international financial reporting standards real quick.

'I was in that position for two years before taking up the role of acting CFO of Anglo Coal when my predecessor moved to London. I was acting for a year before being confirmed in the position. I was in my mid-thirties. This was a defining moment in my professional career, as it felt like I had arrived.'

Mohammed recalls that he had influential sponsors and mentors at Anglo, such as Norman Mbazima, the then CEO of the global coal business, and Ben Magara, then CEO of the South African operation.

'Not long after, Anglo went through a restructure and they split the business into thermal coal and metallurgical coal. It was a harrowing period, because I was not sure whether I would still have a job. I remember boarding a flight to London to meet with [Anglo CEO] Cynthia Carroll about my fate in the company. To my delight, I was appointed CFO of Anglo American Thermal Coal. It was phenomenal and marked the beginning of a new chapter.'

Taking up the CFO role taught Mohammed a lot about people, corporate politics and leadership in general.

'Early on in my career, we rolled up our sleeves and did everything ourselves. Over time, I realised you need to set expectations upfront and deliver by empowering others. First you ensure that you pick the right team members. Then you provide them with the necessary resources so that they can do what is required of them, while regularly checking in on progress to determine whether things are on track. Finally, when holding people to account, do not underestimate the power of performance management and development systems.'

Mohammed, a young executive from Durban, was CFO of a subsidiary of a large, listed mining company. Mining bosses are tough, and he initially felt out of his depth and, sometimes, unwelcome. Nothing that he had done in the past had prepared him for this role.

'I had to work hard at winning them over. I made them understand that my only intention was to move the businesses forward, and to always have their backs. Whenever there was a successful outcome, I made sure the relevant mine manager or general manager got the credit. As a result, I had made more friends than enemies in the business by the time I left in 2011, having learnt how humility helps you accomplish big things.'

ILLOVO SUGAR AND MASSMART

A lot of empowerment deals in South Africa have been unsuccessful. Mohammed believes that true empowerment happens through mentoring and sponsoring young talent and guiding them through the ranks to top management and ownership. This was his experience at both Anglo American and Illovo Sugar.

'I was head-hunted to join Illovo Sugar as CFO in 2011. The idea of joining a listed company with 80% of its operations in Africa appealed to me. It was also an entity that was the subsidiary of a company listed on the FTSE 100 [Financial Times Stock Exchange 100 Index], which I found attractive. Some people thought I was moving backwards, but that could not be further from the truth. It was an opportunity to build some muscle in my career that I didn't have at that point, as I would be exposed to minority shareholders, investor roadshows, external reporting and, most importantly, managing my own balance sheet across six African countries.'

Mohammed brought operational finance experience to the business. He implemented several changes, including recruiting locals to take up the financial director roles in the various African jurisdictions, positions held by expatriates at the time. This was important, as local leadership was critical in establishing helpful relationships with governments and other stakeholders. He also streamlined reporting, strengthened risk management practices, improved the balance sheet and free cash flow generation, reset the cost base and developed talent that has continued to excel in the business.

'Illovo Sugar was a holistic experience. I chaired audit committees in all the various countries and was involved with many aspects of the business, including expansion of plants, investor relations and driving shareholder value. In 2016, Associated British Foods [ABF] decided to increase its shareholding from 51% to 100%. As the largest sugar industry contributor in the ABF group, working on the offer to minority shareholders was a significant exercise and I'm quite proud of the role I had in the transaction.'

Mohammed built 'a world-class finance function' at Illovo, Gavin Dagleish recalls. It had emerged as the best in the ABF group by the time Mohammed left in 2019, prompting a feeling that he had done all that he needed to do at Illovo. His decision to move to Massmart was born from a desire for a new challenge.

'Illovo was like a family to me and I was happy to leave knowing that I'd left it in good shape and in good hands, with a healthy balance sheet and highly talented people that were up to the task. Massmart presented me with the prospect of a different experience in a larger organisation. Two weeks after I joined the company, the then CEO resigned, which was an additional challenge given that the company was struggling financially.'

Mitchell Slape joined Massmart as CEO in September 2019 and Mohammed and he were charged with crafting a turnaround plan.

'Together with the executive team, we developed an ambitious turnaround plan in nine weeks. It was a visionary, necessary and truly transformative exercise – by far the most difficult task I've ever undertaken. In the end, we came up with a plan that is achievable and addresses all the areas of the business that we need to fix. At the heart of it is a cost reset of R1.9 billion, which will require changing the business model from a federated enterprise to more of a centralised one and folding four independent business units into two divisions, namely retail and wholesale.'

The plan went live in January 2020 and it was well received by the market. Nine months later, the company has seen the share price appreciate by about 60% – green shoots starting to emerge from a performance perspective.

'We still have a lot of work to do in the next 18 months, but I believe we're on track. The extensive change management has tested us all at times. But the good thing is that we've had strong support from the holding company, Walmart. The COVID-19 pandemic and the subsequent lockdown has had a devastating effect on our cash flows. We lost R4.7 billion in sales during the first nine weeks of lockdown, but I think we've recovered well. Through managing expenses and working capital better and rental relief from landlords, our debt levels were only marginally higher at the end of June [2020].'

For now, Mohammed is focused on completing the turnaround plan; what he will be up to after that he's not sure yet.

'I actually don't make long-term professional plans, which is funny because I always emphasise long-term planning to others – including when I talk to my daughters, Almira, Inaam and Johara. I try to make sure that I'm sufficiently challenged in what I'm doing and try my best to overcome those challenges, focusing on continuing to develop and staying relevant. I believe that opportunities will come my way and I will chose the right one when it presents itself; sometimes having a big plan can be counterproductive because you become obsessed about achieving the plan. By contrast, if you work hard and enjoy what you do, that in itself will open up the right opportunity and define your next move.'

NOPASIKA LILA

The would-be pianist striking an empowering tune

— INTERVIEW: APRIL 2021 —

One day on her way to work, Nopasika Lila noticed a young boy selling newspapers at a street corner she often passed. At the time she was
working at the Eskom Pension and Provident Fund in Bryanston. Heavy
traffic permitted her to roll down the window and strike up a conversation. She learnt that he was Moses, a 19-year-old in the body of a much
younger adolescent who had just finished high school.

She also heard that Moses' parents had passed away about six years
before and that his sister had paid for his schooling. However, after he
matriculated, she told him it was time for him to find a job and fend for
himself. Nopasika, today group financial director at Barloworld, decided
to take him under her wing. These days, Moses works at a mid-tier audit
firm and is on the verge of qualifying as a chartered accountant.

'Everybody has unlimited abundance that can be nurtured to full
bloom,' Nopasika says, explaining her yearning to mentor. 'The problem
is that our socialisation is flawed, making us believe that we are lesser
beings. Most people have the potential to be very successful, as long as
they have the right attitude. I'm not where I am because I'm better than
anybody else. I'm here because I was fortunate to have opportunities
that others did not.'

Karabo is another example of a life that was changed forever after

Barloworld's Nopasika Lila (*Photo: Austin Malema*)

an encounter with Nopasika. In 2013, Karabo was jobless, with only a matric certificate to her name, when she got a two-day temp job as a personal assistant to Nopasika at the Eskom Pension and Provident Fund. On her second – and last – day, Nopasika had a long chat with her about her future.

The conversation led to Nopasika calling the human resources department to enquire about jobs at the fund. Eventually Karabo was appointed permanently as Nopasika's assistant, a role in which she had the opportunity to experience things such as attending board meetings. Karabo says: 'What I found intriguing about Nopasika is that when she asked me about my situation, it seemed that it was a learning experience for her rather than the judgemental approach I usually encountered. Her curiosity about me made me curious about myself. Also, she believed in me and she challenged me. I accepted the challenge and promised myself that this would be the last time I worked as a personal assistant.'

Karabo completed her undergraduate degree during the three years she worked for Nopasika. Today, ten years later, she has completed an honours degree, is busy completing a master's degree in ICT (information and communications technology) policy and regulations, and runs her own business.

'Besides being a good coach, Nopasika is a great motivator who encourages employees to think like owners and empowers us to do the things we enjoy doing,' wrote colleague Cynthia Makoatsane in 2012 when she nominated Nopasika for the Boss of the Year award. 'She provides direction and inspires our goals by instilling passion about the vision and mission of the organisation. She establishes an environment conducive to continuous improvement, both personally and professionally.'

Nopasika was ranked among the six finalists for the award that year and was also a finalist for the 2016 CFO of the Year award. Giving opportunities to others motivated Nopasika to start the financial management training programme at the Eskom Pension and Provident Fund during her time as CFO.

'It was not easy to get accreditation from the Institute of Chartered Accountants to offer training contracts to aspiring CAs. I had to study to qualify as an assessor and also put together the required work streams that candidates would need to complete. But it was one of the most rewarding times of my career to see staff members who had given up hope of becoming CAs go through the programme and qualify.'

Nopasika's own journey into the world of accounting was initially a very reluctant one. 'I believe that my family tricked me into becoming a chartered accountant!' Nopasika writes on the website CFO South Africa.

'My older sister, Nomfundo, studied to become a chartered accountant while I played the piano and dreamed of studying music. My family advised that I should be cautious not to confuse a hobby for a career and, in retrospect, they were absolutely right. I've thoroughly enjoyed my career, but I've also made time for my love of music, road running and other interests.'

Nopasika has no regrets about becoming an accountant. Looking back, she feels she is making a much broader contribution to economic growth through being in the finance field than she would have if she had pursued music.

Nopasika's mother was a great influence, and some of the lessons she passed on as Nopasika was growing up have enabled her to become the financial leader she is today. 'One thing she always said is that we should aspire to be ourselves and not try to be like other people. If you try to be like somebody else, the best you can do is become a good imitation of them – and that will never be as good as the original you. This is why I emphasise authenticity; I portray the real me to my colleagues and expect the same from them.'

As a high school student, Nopasika remembers being told that accounting was a difficult field and that those who were studying to become accountants were part of an elite group.

'Initially I was overwhelmed with it all, but over time I succeeded. My confidence grew and I've learnt to be a lot more decisive, deliberate and immediate in my actions. After completing articles, I joined Old Mutual in 2001 and moved to the Public Investment Corporation (PIC) four years later, serving as the Head of Compliance and Corporate Governance.'

Nopasika had always wanted to try out being an entrepreneur. After setting up the division at the PIC, she left in 2006 to join four professional women in establishing Astute Intellect, a financial services company that offered services such as asset management, governance and compliance, and audits.

She ran Astute for nearly five years. Why did she leave? Because having previously learnt to speak Mandarin, she now wanted to learn how to read and write it. So she spent a year at a university in Taipei doing exactly that. As a matter of interest, she speaks German, and the only South African languages she doesn't speak are Xitsonga and Tshivenda.

MANAGING OTHERS' ASSETS

Nopasika had been with the Eskom Pension and Provident Fund since 2010, first as CFO and then, from April 2018, as CEO. The fund is one of the largest retirement funds in South Africa, managing more than R145 billion in assets and over 95 000 members.

'When I took over as CEO, our slogan was "Invested in our members". So we focused on our members and transformation. We adopted three E's in achieving these objectives: empowerment, education and evolution of the organisation. In essence, the plan was to empower and educate our employees to better serve our members, while at the same time ensuring that the fund would evolve and adapt to a changing environment.'

Managing others' assets has been a big part of Nopasika's career. I ask her about the reason for her interest in this aspect of financial management.

'The pension and asset management space is quite powerful. Most listed companies are owned by pension contributors and many of these people do not understand how retirement funding works. It fascinated me and I wanted to understand that world. The guiding principle is that fund managers are entrusted by people to make the best of their hard-earned money to safeguard their livelihoods; that's a profound responsibility.'

She goes on to say that managers intentionally have to live up to this position of trust, because for many, their pension is all they have when they retire. 'Because you need to safeguard the assets entrusted to you, your investment strategy and philosophy have to be targeted towards sustainable returns. It's a serious matter to be able to guarantee people that their money will be safe and that it will sustain them in retirement.'

Asked about advice on personal finance, Nopasika urges people to understand their payslips.

'You need to understand how much you're spending on immediate gratification and how much you're investing for later. Look at things such as your medical aid; are you taking the highest package, of which you might not be using all the benefits, or can you downgrade and invest that money elsewhere? Also, the less you save, the more tax you pay, so consider investing more in your retirement, beyond just the minimum your employer is deducting for your pension.'

She laments the fact that people are not taught to start investing early enough. 'The sooner you invest, the more you will have later. I find people even make the mistake of cashing in their pensions when they move from one employer to another. This results in them getting taxed now and the portion that goes to tax could have remained in the fund to give them a much bigger return later. People only start thinking about saving later in life when they realise they need to put away something for their retirement. Yet if they started saving small amounts at the beginning of their career, they would have made so much over time.'

She's right. According to Allan Gray's online investment calculator, you would have an investment worth R4.4 million if you saved R500 a month over 40 years in a fund that promises 6% yearly growth.

'It's amazing what power starting to save early can have, but unfortunately most people seem to be too nonchalant and don't take it seriously. Some people think "What if I save so much and get hit by a bus tomorrow before enjoying my money?" But by not saving, you're losing money to tax anyway, so why take the chance? Saving also does help in the immediate sense, because you can use your annuity as security to buy the things you want today, like a house for example.'

MOVE TO BARLOWORLD

We switch gears to discuss why Nopasika left Eskom's pension fund to take up the role of group financial director at Barloworld.

'I like to take a sabbatical every five years. When I took over the CEO role at the fund, I had not taken my customary break and after a while, I felt that I needed it. So I resigned in March 2019. I was thinking I would be off work for about a year, but the CEO of Barloworld convinced me to take up the role in August.'

Barloworld is an industrial processing, distribution and service company focused on leading international brands. The divisions of the group span equipment (earthmoving equipment and power systems), automotive services (car rental, motor retail, fleet services, used vehicles and disposal solutions), logistics (transport management, supply chain optimisation and freight-forwarding solutions) and consumer industries (starch and glucose).

Nopasika was not looking for an operational role when she was invited for an interview at Barloworld. 'I thought I was going to get a role that was suited to what I had been doing – investments. But the CEO, Dominic Sewela, planted a seed in my mind that I found exciting. All along I've been on the investment side, where I had to make decisions about investing in companies. The management of those companies usually need to sell me their story to convince me the investment is worth it. Now, for the first time, I'm on the other side of the table, where I need to develop and execute strategies that will convince investors that we will grow their money.'

Nopasika says although she now has a more complete picture of the business world, the move has not always been easy. 'It's very, very challenging! Operations are demanding on a daily basis. The level of managing the balance sheet, including cash movement between divisions, requires you to be on your toes. Cash is king and your stakeholders increase so much more. You have to make friends with bankers and asset managers, who provide finance, because your needs are so much more on this side of the table.'

Excellent communication skills are needed for engaging with so many stakeholders. 'You need to have good negotiation skills when engaging banks so that you can get finance on terms that are beneficial to the company. This means that you need to sell your strategy to investors effectively.'

Barloworld is a multinational company, with various businesses across Africa, Europe and Australia. Nopasika's first challenge was managing treasuries in different jurisdictions. 'You can imagine negotiating with banks outside of South Africa, where even the language is different. It's not easy to bridge that cultural divide. Barloworld is also on a growth trajectory, which means mergers and acquisitions are on the cards. So, my job has ended up being a "super function" because beyond finance, I actively have to take part in investor relations, information technology, legal aspects and risk management.'

ON FORMULATING STRATEGY AND HANDLING CRISIS

I ask Nopasika what she thinks makes a good business strategy.

'To start with, a strategy has to be simple and easy to work with. It should not require long explanations before people can understand what you're committing to deliver. It's easy to have lots of words describing a strategy, but it isn't worth much if it's not easy to understand and doesn't spell out the practical steps needed to make it work.

'A good strategy needs a clear direction so that it can be applied throughout the organisation. It is also important that all employees embrace the strategy and understand how their roles contribute to its delivery. It should be a business story with clear milestones and timelines.'

From her time as an investor, she says, she looked at things like whether the strategy had a short-term or long-term view and whether the business was an innovative leader or an industry follower.

'Some companies were not investable because they did not fit within our guardrails – for example, where returns were too small or when they did not invest enough in environmental monitoring, social impact and corporate governance. There were also industries such as tobacco, which we chose not to invest in.'

Nopasika counts herself fortunate to have joined Barloworld at a time when they were reviewing their strategy, because it has given her the opportunity to contribute to its formulation. She shares that they focused on three key aspects, namely, exploiting each business's full potential; identifying opportunities for expansion in each segment; and considering requirements for growing their aspired value.

The Barloworld strategy is well thought out. But as heavyweight boxer Mike Tyson once said about an opponent's fight plan, 'Everyone has a plan until they get punched in the mouth'. Like most companies, that punch came when the COVID-19 pandemic hit in 2020, resulting in a 17% decline in Barloworld's revenues for the year.

Nopasika Lila's independent thinking, courage and spirit of adventure (which takes her skydiving and racing cars on ice) are exactly what is needed to face the sorts of challenges the COVID-19 pandemic has thrown at corporates.

'You might think that I would see the pandemic as a lowlight. But for me, the unusual or unfamiliar is an opportunity to do things differently and to grow. Over the years, I've learnt to be comfortable with uncertainty and ambiguity. Stay calm and centred, take time to reflect, try to understand the new situation and then devise a plan.'

Having been in her role at Barloworld for only a few months when South Africa went into a hard lockdown in March 2020, she says she had to learn to supervise remotely in a business that was relatively new to her. 'Among the many lessons I learnt while navigating the COVID-19 crisis, the one that stood out most was having to be decisive, put my trust in people and empower them. It was satisfying to be able to harness the power of collective wisdom by encouraging people who kept quiet in meetings to speak out and share what were often brilliant ideas, and to challenge when they didn't agree with something.'

Not afraid of challenges and always willing to give others an opportunity in life, Nopasika inspires in the way she leads both businesses and people.

ASPEN PHARMACARE

SEAN CAPAZORIO

Tsunami survivor weathering corporate storms

— INTERVIEW: MARCH 2021 —

Fill a bowl with water. Then drop a rock into it. What happens? Better yet, bang the bowl against the table with force and see the effect.

Now scale it up. Imagine an obese man running towards a pool, leaping high and grabbing his knees while dropping towards the water. Splash! The perfect cannon ball, causing a big wave to splash over the edge of the pool.

The same happens when an underwater earthquake occurs. But imagine a ripple effect so extensive that you see violent waves chasing towards you, while you scramble desperately to get yourself and your pregnant wife away from the unforgiving force of the harsh, dark water.

That was Sean Capazorio's experience on Thailand's Phi Phi islands in December 2004, when a devastating tsunami hit. Journalist Clifford Coonan described it as a scene from the film *Apocalypse Now,* saying it was as if 'a village had been picked up and dropped by an angry giant'. Over 4 000 people are estimated to have died.

On that fateful day, Sean and his wife, Lindsay, were enjoying a stroll down a scenic street when the water swept them up within seconds of making landfall. Unable to breathe or speak, they held on to each other for as long as they could before being separated by the force of the waves.

Sean felt like he was a helpless raft in a raging river. He grabbed onto what he could find, first a telephone pole and then later the top of a

175

coconut tree. In the aftermath, once the water had receded, he faced the longest ten minutes of his life, running around and shouting Lindsay's name like a lost child, the sight of dead bodies lying on the streets fuelling his worst fears.

Thankfully, she had managed to grab onto the roof of a shop where she held on tightly until some locals reached her and pulled her out above the mayhem. Their joy was unconfined when they were reunited.

Sean was quite ill afterwards, suffering from leptospirosis, having swallowed contaminated water during the ordeal. He made a full recovery and six months after leaving the island, the couple celebrated the birth of a healthy baby boy.

'The experience is pivotal to my approach in the corporate environment,' Sean says. 'When faced with crisis, I always ask myself if it's worse than nearly drowning in a tsunami. It never is. And if I survived that, I can survive pretty much anything.'

One such crisis came in September 2018. Reuters carried the headline announcing that Aspen's share price had tumbled more than 35% after it posted full-year results that sparked concerns about its debt levels and sale of its baby formula business.

The memory causes Sean to sigh. 'We've put in a lot of work to restructure the business and the market is responding well to the changes. When faced with crisis, my approach is not to sweat the small stuff but rather prioritise.

'It's important to attend to the key challenges first; you should break down the problem into small pieces.' It's an approach he learnt from endurance sports. (Sean has completed the 109-kilometre Cape Town Cycle Tour 21 times.)

'When going up Chapman's Peak Drive, I break it down into a number of hills and focus on completing each small hill, one at a time. This helps keep me calm as opposed to getting stressed thinking about how far the ultimate peak is.'

MANAGING MONEY MADE FROM MEDICINES

Sean's journey to becoming a CFO began at Dawnview High in Germiston, with the inspiration of his accounting teacher, Mr Tonetti.

Aspen Pharmacare's Sean Capazorio *(Photo: Aspen)*

'I wanted to become an accountant or a doctor,' Sean recalls. 'But clinical medicine was going to be a struggle, given that I faint at the sight of blood. So accounting was really my only option. In an interesting twist of fate, I work for a pharmaceutical company, so I haven't totally escaped the idea of working in medicine.'

After finishing his accounting studies at the University of the Witwatersrand in 1986, he joined Coopers & Lybrand for articles. He subsequently worked as a manager at the firm and then went to the military for a year of compulsory national service. In 1993, he joined the Unisys Corporation, an IT company, where he worked as a management accountant for three years before joining SA Druggists.

'Completing an advanced certificate in taxation at UNISA [the University of South Africa] was helpful in getting me into an operational role at SA Druggists. I've always enjoyed operational finance and that aspect of my job description remained when Aspen purchased the pharmaceutical business of SA Druggists. The post-merger shift in culture also suited me, seeing that Aspen had an entrepreneurial approach compared with the rigid and bureaucratic style of SA Druggists.'

Sean served as the finance director of the South African leg of Aspen's business from 2000 to 2004. In 2005 he moved to Durban, where he worked as a group business analyst. He was appointed as the group's CFO in 2009.

I ask him what is so special about Aspen that he has chosen to spend more than two decades at the company.

'We call it the University of Aspen because we learn so much every day,' he laughs. 'Each year is different from the one before. It's been a roller coaster with so many acquisitions and disposals across different jurisdictions. There's never been a boring moment in this place!'

EFFECTIVE TEAMS

Aspen Pharmacare has 9 800 employees globally and operates in 150 countries. It is the biggest pharmaceutical company in Africa and its turnover has grown from R1 billion to R38 billion in the past 20 years. As group financial officer, Sean is responsible for over 200 finance professionals and deals with a myriad of tasks, including group reporting, commercial finance, tax, treasury and project finance.

I ask him about his approach to leading such a big team of people.

'My attention to detail is quite high. Thanks to my extensive experience, I have good insight into how things should work. That said, I'm not an autocratic type of leader. I expect people to manage themselves; my role is to coach, mentor and guide them.'

'I am also emphatic about integrity. I tell my guys that without integrity, the numbers mean absolutely nothing.'

One of Sean's key lessons over the years has been to lean on the people around him as much as possible. 'We all take on too much sometimes and one of the best ways to handle key problems is to delegate.

In that way everybody shares in seeking a solution, not just the person at the top.'

For Sean, personnel gaps – whether upwards or downwards – represent particularly challenging moments. 'Our deputy CEO called us out of the blue once and told us he would be on medical leave for two months. I had to take on some of his tasks, which was quite demanding. There was also a time when a few key staff members resigned to seek new career opportunities. I realised just how critical they were because the gap they left was significant.'

It is heartbreaking when you invest a lot of time in people and then they leave the company, Sean laments.

'The younger generation tend to move around much more than some of us older professionals. It re-emphasises the need to keep your people motivated. But even that is sometimes not enough, so you need to be prepared to deal with their departure and carry on.'

When it comes to managing a team, another important aspect for Sean is early detection. 'I don't like late surprises. I always tell my team they should not be afraid of telling me something I might not want to hear. I would rather know about a problem early, so that we can flag it quickly and get it dealt with. It's actually part of the culture at Aspen; we have a flat structure that allows everyone accountability and responsibility. We also try to be proactive in anticipating problems, so that solutions are devised way in advance.'

He admits that they do not always get it right. 'We had quite a big investment in Venezuela. When the country started to implode, we had to learn about hyperinflation accounting very quickly and report accordingly. But when inflation hits 10 000%, it becomes ridiculous and the numbers are meaningless. At some point, the government allowed pharmaceutical companies to take money out at a very favourable exchange rate, but even that did not last long. In the end, we had to write off the entire investment. It was quite painful.'

The Venezuelan experience is an exception to an otherwise long story of success for Aspen, and Sean stresses that being proactive is an important lesson for any professional. 'For example, think outside your academic background and professional training. If you're an accountant having to think through a problem, don't just approach it like the average accountant, hypnotised by numbers. Put yourself in the operational manager's shoes and try to think about various alternatives for solving the problem.'

He also advises younger professionals to be the captain of their own ship. 'You should not wait for people to give you things to do. And don't focus only on finance; broaden your horizons. Keep your finance core but expand your knowledge base.

'The way I learnt over the years was by getting involved in other areas of the business: going down to the manufacturing floor, understanding the supply chain, taking an interest in legal contracts ... that's how you understand the business as a whole.'

Sean says he sees too many 25-year-olds entering the corporate world expecting opportunities to fall in their lap. 'They arrive with all this deep technical knowledge from university and expect that to be enough to propel their careers forward. You need more; you need perseverance going through tough times, understanding what you're doing and believing in what you're trying to achieve. Being well rounded will help you see beyond the details to appreciate the bigger picture.'

When it comes to recruitment, Sean looks for honest, technically and commercially sound, energetic and forward-thinking self-starters, he said in an interview with CFO South Africa. Good communication is also important, as people from different cultures make up Aspen's staff.

Sean undertakes coaching as an informal, on-the-job process. It is essential, because 'the more you teach others, the less you have to do yourself'.

STRATEGIC THINKING

'Plan your work and work your plan,' Sean advises. 'Don't do things on an ad-hoc basis. Plan your day, your month, your year and so on. It helps to give you and your team structure, which is something they will enjoy. It doesn't help to tell people to do one thing on one day and a different thing the next day. You will lose people along the way if you don't have a clear plan and strategy.'

A good strategy is a simple one, he says. Something too complex just won't work.

'It's one of the things I've learnt from our CEO, Stephen Saad. He is the master of simplification. He knows how to strip a business to its key components and isolate those that add value from those that don't. In that way we can identify the ones we should best discontinue or dispose of because they're not adding value to our portfolio, and rather focus our efforts on changing one or two things in those not doing so well to let them thrive.'

Aspen has an organic approach to growth. 'We look at creating and optimising value based on our stated end game. A strategy should also be dynamic. You cannot put something in a book and say: "That's our strategy; we're sticking to it." As opportunities and risks arise, your strategy needs to change.'

During its early life, Aspen was very much a generic drug business. (A generic drug is one that contains the same chemical substance as a drug that was originally protected by a patent.) The manner in which the company moved away from its focus on generics illustrates the dynamic nature of their strategy.

'We realised that if we remained in generics, we would become a commodity-based business facing stiff competition. That's why we went into sterile focus brands, which include anaesthetics and thrombosis products. We invested a lot of time and effort but the returns were not immediately apparent to investors – we had to convince them to support us through that journey. Looking back, it was the right move, as we are in a much better space than those that stayed in generics.'

It has taken a long time to reshape the business and get the capacity and manufacturing strategies in place. Patience is therefore important in achieving the stated outcome of a strategy.

'You also need to be sure that you have the right people with you to make your strategy work. Someone may be very good at one stage of a strategy, but when it gets to the next, a different skillset is needed. So, you need to have the right people at the right time.'

HIGHLIGHTS

A memorable achievement for Sean was securing a manufacturing deal with a US-based company in 2009 to manufacture eye drops. It was a noteworthy success given that they managed to convince the company to move the manufacture of their largest brand – Murine Clear Eyes – from the US to Port Elizabeth (now Gqeberha).

One day, while on holiday in the US with his family, CEO Stephen Saad wandered into a pharmacy. On a shelf he found Murine Clear Eyes, with the words 'Made In Port Elizabeth' written on the box. It's indicative of Aspen's growth story: from a converted house in Durban to the largest pharmaceutical company in the southern hemisphere and the ninth largest generics company in the world.

At the time of our interview, Aspen was in advanced discussions with Johnson & Johnson (J&J) to manufacture their COVID-19 vaccine candidate. Aspen expected to produce up to 300 million doses in Gqeberha over time, to be packaged as part of J&J's global inventory. 'The arrangement has done a great deal for our reputation, as we will be playing a pivotal part in addressing a pandemic that has claimed many lives,' said Sean.

As the finance function is fundamental to the Aspen success story, Sean and his team should share in the credit for the group's progression.

In 2018, Sean received the Finance Transformation Award from CFO South Africa, acknowledging Aspen's globalisation journey.

'We had to work out a method for reporting our numbers on a look-through basis, allowing us to report the performance of the group without the legal-entity noise. Imagine a product being made in the US, going through the Netherlands and ending up being sold in Brazil. That's a lot of jurisdictions with a lot of companies. We had to design a system that tells you the exact profit you were making from that product by decluttering the entities.'

Sean mentions that another innovative step was coming up with a 'constant exchange rate' for reporting purposes. 'We have multiple currencies impacting our business and if you get caught up in the changes happening to each of them, it becomes difficult to determine the true performance of each region. We go back to the source currency for each of our inputs and convert them at the applicable rate, which we keep constant so that the currency fluctuations do not detract from determining the performance.'

A third motivation for the award was the effort in integrating the finance functions of the company in Europe and Asia following a string of acquisitions undertaken by the group.

Sean was also a finalist for the 2021 CFO of the Year award.

I conclude our interview by asking him where he sees himself next. 'CEO perhaps?' I venture.

He laughs heartily.

'No, no, no … I think I'm too conservative to be the CEO. CEOs generally have a much higher risk appetite and as a finance person, I view my role as balancing such risk.'

NISHLAN SAMUJH

Tending trillions in tumultuous times

— INTERVIEW: AUGUST 2021 —

When Investec CFO Nishlan Samujh puts his mind to something, there's no stopping him. Growing up in the hilly suburb of Overport in Durban, Nishlan looked up to many successful individuals in his extended family. One of his cousins, an accountant, always had the demeanour of a consummate professional and was admired by the entire family.

Nishlan desperately wanted to be like him, and he started investigating how to become a chartered accountant in high school – he even documented this as his career plan in his diary. Passing his matric examinations with an A average earned him a 100% fee exemption for his first year's accounting studies at the University of Durban-Westville (today the University of KwaZulu-Natal). This financial relief was crucial, as his mother was a single parent who had to work long hours as a seamstress at a clothing company to provide for Nishlan and his brother.

A bursary from Sasol later allowed him to complete his degree and he joined the company's auditors, KPMG, in Durban for articles after graduating among the top of his class in 1996. 'Joining the workplace was exciting. It was a quantum leap going from theoretical lessons at university to auditing companies in practice. It's one thing to get the audit file done, but quite another to grasp the reason why we're doing

Investec's Nishlan Samujh *(Photo: Karolina Komendera)*

what we're doing. I was quite interested in the latter,' says Nishlan.

During an articles contract, trainees learn the ropes in accounting and auditing disciplines, but, in most firms, there is little exposure to taxation. Seeking to have a more holistic understanding of the accounting qualification, Nishlan pursued a higher diploma in taxation at his alma mater, graduating in 1997.

After completing his articles contract in 1999, Nishlan joined Sasol in Johannesburg as a corporate reporting accountant. At the time, the chemicals company had invested heavily in research and development, which fascinated him. Despite this interest, he was still finding his professional niche and felt Sasol might not be the right place.

JOINING INVESTEC

After a series of interviews, Nishlan was offered a financial reporting accountant position at Investec in January 2000. (The bank also agreed to compensate Sasol for Nishlan's bursary.)

'For some reason I was attracted to financial services,' he recalls. 'It was not ideal for me to leave Sasol so quickly, but I think that it was best for us all. Employees should be placed in organisations they are passionate about and do things that truly engage them. Often people stay in organisations out of a sense of obligation, which is virtuous, but you also need to ensure you're taking the right steps to find what suits you.'

Nishlan's responsibilities initially involved technical accounting and consolidation financial reporting. Over time, he built networks within the bank, which put him in contact with influential colleagues and exposed him to different transactions. He saw exciting changes at the bank during his first two years, including a black economic empowerment deal and listing on the London Stock Exchange.

'As part of the finance team, I learnt a lot in watching these processes unfold,' says Nishlan. 'Other transactions included the acquisition of the financial services and insurance businesses of Fedsure and the establishment of Investec Employee Benefits. As a young man coming into a company doing all these things, I was enthralled.'

In January 2010, Nishlan was appointed as the head of the finance function for the South African operation, and six years later he assumed the role of group CFO.

'When I look back at how I became a financial director, I consider myself very fortunate because I had so many mentors who pushed me to test boundaries. They helped me identify my strengths and weaknesses. Investec's environment also encourages people to take ownership and focus on outcomes, which helped prepare me for a leadership role.'

Overt guidance from colleagues exposed him to different ways of thinking through challenges. This experience included the opportunity to interact with the London office, which gave him international exposure and had a significant influence on his career.

He also believes he was at the right place at the right time. When Steve Binnie, the former head of finance and one of his mentors, left the company, Nishlan was well positioned to step up. He was appointed as an executive director in 2019, after the bank decided to transition from its founding leaders to the next generation of management.

By the time Nishlan turns 50, he will have been at Investec for half his life. He loves the organisation because it resonates with what he stands for: delivering impactful and sustainable solutions for its clients. It is a company that rewards those who are willing to take the steps necessary to grow their careers.

'It's not an organisation that has a set path for employee progression along clear-cut steps and ladders. Your growth comes from how you interact, how you network and how you effectively make an impact in the organisation. I think the kind of people development we foster is magical.'

HIGHS AND LOWS OF CAREER AND LIFE

Becoming an executive director on the group board has been one of the highlights of Nishlan's career. It gives him a completely different lens on the organisation and what he does. 'But I also count as highs all the times that I've been allowed to perform at my fullest – during the various cycles the company has gone through and I have been able to participate in executing key objectives and processes.'

A low point in his life was his mother's passing when he was 22 years old. 'This was just as I was launching into a new phase of my life and my career,' Nishlan says. 'It pains me that she's no longer around to share in my personal and professional success. I remember her as someone who dedicated her life to ensuring that my brother and I had bright futures. All we can do now is to continue on the path she set us on and live life positively in her memory.'

While he might not have grown up in a wealthy household, what they lacked financially was made up for in a rich community experience in their segregated Indian community. His memories of his childhood include happy times playing cricket in the streets, studying with the neighbours' children and boyhood adventures from their neighbourhood all the way to the Durban city centre.

Like any other professional, Nishlan has experienced lows in the workplace, too. He recalls one incident when he was called into a meeting and challenged for not seeing the big picture on a project. 'It was tough because I was put on the spot to explain what I thought was the crux of the problem we were facing. It took me a few days to get to the bottom of why the meeting went down that way. At the time it felt like a personal attack, but in hindsight it was a lesson in leadership, because it was a worthwhile challenge to push myself.'

On that note, Nishlan explains that constructive criticism is vital and that it is important that you should teach yourself to pause and listen to others. 'I'm the kind of character who is continually in solve mode – I want to race to find solutions. As a result, it's quite possible to miss the warnings from others who see things through a different lens. The importance of listening cannot be overstated.'

If Nishlan could go back 20 years, he says, he would participate in more initiatives early on in his career. As a self-confessed introvert, there were often times when he could have spoken up and contributed to solving problems, but he chose not to. He advises young professionals to make their voices heard, rather than merely float through discussions at work.

To be successful, Nishlan urges professionals to be honest with themselves and to trust in their abilities. 'You should also be ready to put in the hard yards. Don't frown upon the tough phases of life, because challenges are the things that build you. When you're young, you don't have much patience. You're eager to touch success, yet accomplishment takes time, vision, tenacity and being alive to the world around you.'

LEADERSHIP AND MANAGEMENT

Nishlan reminds the younger generation of business professionals that management is never looking only for one type of person, and it is best to just be yourself. The most successful teams are those whose members all think differently. 'Don't go to work just for the sake of it; be mindful of the way you show up. Seek to improve, seek to adjust and seek to add value.'

Looking at his finance team, Nishlan can think of several team members whose resignation would cause him sleepless nights. Their corporate knowledge and sense of responsibility make them immensely valuable. That said, he understands that changes in a team are inevitable and that change also has its merits because it injects fresh thinking into the team dynamic.

Investec has a formal mentorship programme, where senior staff get the opportunity to mould mentees. The programme also has a 're-verse mentorship' aspect, with staff providing their perspective of how management is running the organisation.

'I find it beneficial to listen to our people,' Nishlan mentions. 'I'm not the kind of manager to crack the whip and be on people's backs 24/7. I believe giving people space to do their jobs and trusting them is very important. My style is to let someone take ownership, and then give sufficient feedback to help them achieve the set outcomes.'

When it comes to strategy, Nishlan thinks it can be both overplayed and, at times, underplayed. For example, it can happen that a strategy is developed to fit a particular set of conditions, but when those conditions change, the management team is so dedicated to it that they fail to adapt to the new environment. In contrast, the value of strategy can be un-derplayed when companies simply go with the flow. In such an instance they usually lack clear guidelines of what they want to achieve and how they want to get there. 'A good strategy strikes a balance between these two positions,' he says.

Another feature of a good strategy is simplicity, driven by solid knowledge. Strategists must have a deep understanding of their busi-ness landscape and should know their organisation, their capabilities and their market. Challenges are inevitable and leaders need to remain centred and understand what they can control and what they can't.

Nishlan believes handling a crisis requires a pragmatic approach in which you need to take time to evaluate the environment. Acquiring the right tools and developing appropriate skills are important in responding to changes in your environment. 'Always be careful not to get too comfortable, because comfort is the enemy of change. It is important to sit down often and evaluate whether you're moving forward.

'A crisis like the COVID-19 pandemic forced us to re-examine our processes, particularly the use of technology,' Nishlan explains. 'We all had a virtual meeting app available on our computers as part of a standard software suite, but we weren't using it; now it is essential to our daily work. These are some of the positives that can come out of a crisis, because technology undoubtedly increases our efficiency.'

He adds that he is proud of the finance team's ability to go through an audit and publish financial statements while in hard lockdown. The way in which the company was able to respond to customer and stakeholder needs during lockdown was 'simply amazing'.

Nishlan believes in being responsive to the needs of a company's stakeholders. 'At the start of the 2021 financial year, we embarked on an extensive process to simplify our external reporting,' he writes in the Investec Annual Report 2021. 'This initiative was driven by requests from key Investec stakeholders to provide simplified and more transparent disclosure. During the current year, efforts were focused on the simplicity and relevance of the information provided in the analyst book and to improve the general clarity of the annual report.'

Whereas he always seeks information from different sources, Nishlan confesses that he is 'a terrible reader'. Of the few books he has read recently, he recommends *A Short History of Nearly Everything* by Bill Bryson. It gives a very good perspective of how we got to where we are and what it will take for humanity to progress.

And this, dear reader, is the short history of Nishlan Samujh, the son of a seamstress from Overport, who has gone from writing a career plan in his diary as a young boy to formulating strategy for an institution with over a trillion rands' worth of assets.

REEZA ISAACS

The family man

— INTERVIEW: SEPTEMBER 2021 —

Reeza Isaacs was born to factory-worker parents in District Six, Cape Town, in 1968. The prime location of this vibrant 'mixed' suburb prompted the apartheid government to declare it a 'whites only' area in 1972. At the age of four, Reeza and his family were evicted and moved to Surrey Estate on the Cape Flats.

Growing up in a community of blue-collar workers, Reeza did not have any mentors who could guide him through career choices in professional fields. However, he had heard that a three-year degree in accounting could get you a decent salary, because he wanted to help his family, he decided to go this route.

He reckons he was fortunate to get a bursary from Shell, given that his matric results were average. Like many other coloured, Indian and black students on South African campuses in the volatile political climate that prevailed in the 1980s, his studies had been disrupted by anti-apartheid protests.

He enrolled at the University of Cape Town in 1987 and found the transition to a predominantly white institution very challenging. He was pleasantly surprised when, despite the obstacles, he got good results in his first year and made the Dean's Merit List. He realised he was more than capable of holding his own.

STARTING A CAREER IN AUDITING

During his third year at university, Ernst & Young (today doing business as EY) offered to pay for Reeza's honours studies on condition that he join the firm for articles once he graduated. He joined the company in 1991, working from their Long Street offices in Cape Town.

Reeza recalls a friendly environment that was much less prejudiced than he had expected. Even if not all of the firm's clients believed in the need for transformation in the corporate space, he found the firm quite progressive.

After completing his articles, Reeza was selected to go to the US on a long-term residency programme. For a boy from the jagged tracks of the Cape Flats, it was an 'exciting and strange' experience to spend time with inductees from all parts of the world at the programme's introduction in Florida. He was then posted to New Jersey, where he worked on audits of financial institutions in the Garden State and neighbouring New York.

Despite having an opportunity to extend his stay with the firm in the US, Reeza longed for home and decided to return to Cape Town at the end of his secondment in 1995. Shortly after his arrival, the firm faced a potentially crippling reputational crisis in South Africa after thousands of pensioners lost their investments because of fraud at Masterbond, one of Ernst & Young's audit clients. The scandal led to the departure of many partners and Reeza decided he was going to follow suit.

But while he was still working on his next move, the newly appointed CEO Philip Hourquebie arranged for a meeting with Reeza to tap into his views on the challenges the firm was facing. Philip's vision and determination to change things for the better convinced Reeza to remain with the company as part of the team that would work to restore the firm's reputation.

'In 1999, I was appointed partner and went on to have a nice mix of clients, big companies such as Metropolitan Life, Truworths, BP and Engen. Having Sanlam as a client allowed us to increase the depth of the talent in financial services by incorporating corporate finance professionals and actuaries.'

In 2007, Reeza was asked to head the audit division of the Cape Town firm and three years later he was appointed executive in charge

Woolworths' Reeza Isaacs *(Photo: Woolworths Holdings)*

of the practices in the Western and Eastern Cape. Despite having these management roles, he remained the partner responsible for the audit of several blue-chip companies, including Sanlam, Coronation Fund Managers and Woolworths.

THE WOOLWORTHS WHIRLWIND

'Just as my term as engagement partner at Woolworths was coming to an end, the then CFO of Woolworths retired and I was offered his position. I decided to accept because further promotion within Ernst & Young would have required that I relocate to the head office in Johannesburg. I've always fancied living in Cape Town, given our deep family ties here, and Woolworths is one of only a few listed retailers that operate from the Mother City.'

A move to South Africa's commercial capital might have opened many more lucrative opportunities for Reeza, but he believes 'a united, extended family is much more important than money'. He took up the Woolworths CFO position in June 2013 and shortly afterwards the company decided to acquire the Australian department store David Jones.

Management was excited about the prospect of creating a leading southern hemisphere retailer comprising David Jones and Woolworths, with pro forma combined revenue from 1 151 stores across 16 countries amounting to more than R51 billion. Things started off well in 2015/16, but the Australian investment faced serious headwinds soon after and had to be impaired. Reeza describes it as a 'whirlwind experience, with lots of lessons that no MBA in the world could ever teach'.

'One of the most challenging days was having to go to the CEO's office to inform him that we had no option but to impair our investment in David Jones. It's never fun being the bearer of bad news.'

Despite such difficult moments, Reeza does not let the work get to him. In his view, work is not an end in itself. In life, he is guided by a strong set of beliefs, and the strength he draws from his family is something 'no amount of money can buy'.

'You shouldn't take your work too seriously,' he advises. 'People lose too much sleep over their jobs, as if their day-to-day hustle is something that will bring world peace or put an end to a refugee crisis. Don't stress yourself out, because it's unlikely that people are living or dying on the basis of your decisions.'

To strengthen its balance sheet, the group decided to sell some of its Australian properties. Selling the Elizabeth Street property in Sydney housing David Jones netted R5.6 billion and was part of a process to restructure the group's Australian debt. Things have been demanding in recent times: apart from the sub-par performance of the Australian business, there was also the COVID-19 pandemic to contend with.

'This [was] a period that is unprecedented and most extraordinary in recent memory and indeed in the history of our Group,' Reeza wrote in the Woolworths 2020 Annual Report. 'The extremely challenging trading conditions brought about by the pandemic placed significant pressure on the performance of our discretionary businesses across the Group. However, the exceptional performance of our food business in South Africa and the growth in our online channels underpinned the Group results for the year.'

STRATEGY AND MANAGEMENT

The Australian experience has taught Reeza a few important lessons. For example, when it comes to mergers and acquisitions, the numbers you see on a spreadsheet are often much more attractive than the reality. Companies that embark on acquisitions should keep in mind that post-merger integration is a very difficult process, which should be duly considered before inking a deal.

Reeza also learnt a fair bit about resilience. Being the CFO of one of South Africa's top companies is not for the faint-hearted. During his day in auditing, Reeza was responsible for running a professional practice that was quite collegial. The corporate environment is much tougher and he has seen a number of executives come and go, given the challenges that the retail group faced.

Being persuasive is a critical characteristic for a successful CFO, as you need to put forward convincing arguments to the board, investors and lenders. Yet you should be careful not to lose your values and the essence of who you are in getting desired decisions over the line, Reeza warns. Minimise stress and try to achieve balance by taking breaks and getting enough sleep.

'I have a place at the coast where the family and I escape to as often as possible,' he says. To Reeza, a father of four, it is also important to sustain family and social circles, particularly in times such as those we're going through now, with increased isolation because of the COVID-19 pandemic putting a strain on people's mental health. 'I urge professionals to look after their spiritual well-being and try to have fun at the end of the day,' he advises.

Looking back, Reeza says he doesn't have any career regrets and there's not much he would have done differently, except perhaps venturing into commerce sooner.

When it comes to strategy, Reeza's view is that executives should keep up to date with an ever-changing environment and seek wide-ranging input, including external perspectives. Everyone in the company has to buy in to the strategy, and for that the strategy has to be simple and understandable. 'Clarity about where you're now and where you want to get to will help your team to know what they should focus on,' he says.

Reeza believes by hiring competent people, you won't have to micromanage them. He feels strongly about empowering his team but also giving them the space to make mistakes, and working with them to improve their performance. He stresses that keeping lines of communication open means that if there is bad news, it can be dealt with it as soon as possible.

Reeza admits that he can get impatient when it comes to depending on others. With years of experience, he can spot errors quickly and have a sense of when things are just not stacking up. 'In the corporate space you need to have the capacity for dealing with many things at once and in a short space of time. As a result, you need to plan your time wisely and work smart. The retail environment in particular is very fast paced.'

Looking into the future, Reeza has his mind set on what he calls 'unfinished business' at Woolworths. He is passionate about being part of a team that will leave the company in good standing for the next generation of leaders. A family man through and through, he rushes off from sharing his musings about his corporate life to attend his daughter's art evening at school.

SIMON ADAMS

The achiever who likes to live in the moment

— INTERVIEW: JULY 2021 —

Not all finance is the same or excites him equally, Simon Adams of Nando's South Africa learnt at a young age. This might explain his job hopping in his early twenties and thirties and why, if he had a choice between working in, say, mining or the food industry, he would pick the latter.

Simon is a born achiever, I realised shortly after we both joined the Johannesburg office of RSM Betty & Dickson as article clerks in 2005. He always went further and asked lots of questions to grasp his seniors' expectations. Despite looking young, he was already proving himself to be a talented and reliable team member over whom seniors would haggle when planning staff for their audits. At the 2005 year-end dinner, he was crowned the rookie trainee of the year, leaving the rest of us green with envy at his salary bump as a performance reward.

By late 2007, Simon broke the collective hearts of the RSM partners by announcing that he would be leaving the firm at the end of his contract. They were desperate to make him a manager, but Simon was convinced auditing was not for him. Besides, he had received an offer to join Anglo American, one of the world's largest diversified mining companies, as a strategy accountant.

But what had initially seemed like a dream move did not meet his expectations. 'I didn't feel like I fitted into the organisation,' Simon recalls. 'The work did not resonate with me and because it was still early in my career, it was possible for me to change companies quicker. Going in, I was still quite naïve about accounting in the corporate environment, but I learnt fairly quickly that not all finance is the same. The mining industry just didn't excite me.'

Simon left Anglo after three months. As a young man with no dependants, he was unperturbed about not having permanent employment. He accepted a short-term contract role at Japan Tobacco International (JTI), where his primary responsibility was to assist the financial manager with month-end reporting.

As a devout Christian, was he conflicted about working in a so-called sin industry?

'If you torture the data hard enough, it will confess to anything,' he quotes British economist Ronald Coase. 'Similarly, if you set out to draw a bad parallel with an industry, you will soon succeed. It's easy to find fault anywhere. I now work for a chicken fast-food chain, which many may find inappropriate given the veganism movement. At JTI, I came to appreciate that whereas the eventual consumer might engage in a bad habit, the role the tobacco and other sin industries play in the economy cannot be overstated,' Simon says.

Working at JTI brought Simon a few interesting experiences as a non-smoker. For one, during the 2008 Olympics, when the world was mesmerised by Usain Bolt, the only space at the office with a TV was in the smoking area, which meant sitting in a cloud of secondary smoke if you wanted to watch world records being broken. The company also gave all employees many free cigarette packs. Simon soon became very popular with caddies on the golf course ...

After ten months at the company, Simon secured a permanent role at Entyce Beverages, a division within AVI, in March 2009. His responsibilities included cost and efficiency management under Deepa Sita, currently group CFO at Tiger Brands.

When Sita left Entyce Beverages for Kraft Foods (now known as Mondelēz International), she invited Simon to join her at the company. He duly obliged, taking up the position of financial planning and analysis manager in May 2011.

Nando's SA's Simon Adams *(Photo: Nando's)*

KRAFT FOODS

As a member of the leadership team in the finance function, Simon was involved in integrating two finance teams – those of Kraft Foods and Cadbury – after Cadbury had been taken over by Kraft a year before. Among Sita's responsibilities was Kraft Foods Kenya, which had received negative internal audit reports. This called for a visit from the South African finance leadership team in early 2012 to assess whether the company needed to be dissolved.

Stuck in snail's pace traffic in Nairobi on the way to the hotel after spending time on site, Simon looked outside the window and was enthralled by the spirit and energy of the East African people. He mentioned to Sita that he would be happy to move to Kenya to try and resolve the issues the company was facing. 'Be careful what you wish for,' she warned.

A few weeks later, as they were working late into the night back at the Johannesburg office, Sita called Simon into her office and reminded him of their conversation in Nairobi. She asked him if he was serious about solving their Kenyan problem. Simon replied that nothing had changed. His wife, Sian, was also open to the move, as she had just completed an MBA and was looking forward to some time off to start a family.

While they were planning the move Sian fell pregnant, and many people asked the couple whether this meant they would reconsider the move. 'People have children in Kenya every day,' was their response. They found a good doctor in Nairobi, who delivered the first two of their three children.

'Unlike the conveyer belt 15-minute sessions we had in Johannesburg, Dr Patel would spend the full hour-long consultation with us, just talking about pregnancy and family,' Simon remembers fondly. 'When we first met him, we gave him all our scans from our gynae visits in Johannesburg. He was totally uninterested in them, saying that they didn't use such technology there. Instead he pulled out what looked like a radio from the 1920s and that rusty thing ended up being very accurate about the delivery date!'

As head of finance at Cadbury Kenya, Simon's job was to resolve the company's cash flow problems. They had ordered tons of raw cocoa to manufacture drinking chocolate, but a slowdown in the Kenyan economy, exacerbated by terrorist attacks by Al Shabab, had caused a dip in sales. As a result, the company could not meet their payment obligations, which were largely in foreign currency.

'Fortunately the economy picked up and we were able to trade out of the situation. But the group decided to shut down the manufacturing plant and rather use distributors to push their products in the Kenyan market. One thing I'm proud of is that we gave generous termination packages to the employees, particularly those who had been with the company for many years.'

One of the employees who had been there for decades was Philip Kioko, a shop steward. He walked into Simon's office on his last day to thank him for his contribution. 'He insisted that I must return to the country and promised to organise for a local woman to be my second wife. He was dead serious, and I nearly fell off my chair laughing. I was at pains to explain to him that I came from a different culture and that Sian would not be too pleased with the arrangement.'

BIC AND NANDO'S

Simon resigned from Kraft and the Adams family returned to South Africa early in 2015. A month after their return, Simon took up the role of CFO of the South, East and Central African leg of BIC, a family-controlled company listed on the Paris Stock Exchange and well known for its shavers, lighters and stationery.

'I was blown away by what a nice company BIC was. They have a consolidated revenue of over two billion euros, which could be considered average for a company represented in over 160 countries. But if you consider the fact that they sell small items, it translates to the distribution of millions of units of product. And it's not just the quantity: they consistently exceed the minimum quality standards set by industry.'

Simon enjoyed his role at BIC given how professionally the entity was run. He also got the opportunity to travel across Africa often, which is something he really enjoys. Needless to say he was somewhat reluctant to pick up the call when, just 18 months into the role, a recruiter reached out to him with an offer.

'But when I heard that he was looking for someone for a senior finance role in Nando's South Africa, it was a conversation I had to have. Nando's is a great South African brand with an international presence. What was exciting for me was that it was a change to front-end retail, while the jobs I had been involved in up to that point were largely at the back end of the supply chain and focused on manufacturing and distributing product.'

It is an interesting contrast, because in a manufacturing environment you have relationships with wholesale customers with whom you negotiate inventory orders. As a result, you can plan around your production, deliveries and payment. In the restaurant business, though, you can't expect that a customer who does not eat on one day will come and eat two meals the next day. 'That was a learning curve for me and once I wrapped my head around the accounting processes, managing the finance team became much easier. I have been here almost five years now and all is going well.'

Simon continues to be the achiever I've always known. So it came as no surprise when, in February 2021, CFO South Africa announced that he was a finalist for the Young CFO of the Year award.

SIMON SAYS ...

Simon advises young professionals to determine what drives them. It may sound clichéd, he says, but money is not everything. Yes, it offers financial security, but it's also crucial to figure out as early as possible what other things motivate you. That includes what you want from a company in terms of your time, your expertise, relationships and friendships. For him, for example, a role that promises opportunities to travel and experience different cultures is attractive.

'Try to learn from everybody in your company, not just those higher up in the corporate hierarchy. Everybody has a story and if you care to listen, you'll be surprised at the gems you uncover.' He points out that for accountants in particular there is a marked transition into business; during articles they are working with like-minded peers but when they leave, they are suddenly surrounded by people of all ages who are not all bean-counters. It is important to have your wits about you when you make that change, so that you can adapt to new people and new ways of thinking.

'Youngsters should not be in a hurry to move up the ladder,' Simon cautions. 'While it is nice to get promotions and more responsibility, you should appreciate that there's so much to learn at each stage. Be careful not to jump too quickly in pursuit of a promotional paycheck. But at the same time, be wary of stagnating. If you feel you're no longer adding value in your role, it may be time to consider other opportunities.'

Yet he thinks he has been a bit too linear in his career moves, putting it down to his risk-averse nature. 'In retrospect, I think you should not try and control everything and should occasionally just take a leap of faith, because often times things will not go according to plan, no matter how methodical you try to be.'

For this reason, Simon tries to live in the moment and just enjoy what he is doing, without worrying too much about what is up next. There is a range of possibilities, including seeking further opportunities in the Nando's group, working in a different industry, working in a different country, or assuming a role in broader management.

Although a career in accounting exposes a professional to various business functions, it is important to continue to expand your knowledge. In this regard, Simon is currently undertaking a master's degree with specialisation in corporate strategy. The course is designed to 'help you gain a deep understanding of how organisations need to think about and react to rapidly changing business environments, digital disruption and fast-changing business models'.

Some of the lessons in strategy Simon shares include the art of strategic foresight, scenario planning and the practice of business futures. The COVID-19 pandemic, which few saw coming, is a classic example of a possible disruption that future strategies should consider.

He also believes a strategy should span all facets of the company to avoid treating different functions as silos. It should go beyond the numbers and be centred around the problems the business looks to solve – which for Nando's, involve offering healthy but tasty fast food. It is the solutions that the company provides and how effectively it solves problems that make the entity and its strategy relevant.

YURESH MAHARAJ

A crusader for financial freedom

— INTERVIEW: MAY 2021 —

As the child of a teacher who had to make do with a modest salary, Liberty's financial director, Yuresh Maharaj, did not grow up with the proverbial golden spoon in the mouth. But the one thing his father, Ram, promised to give him and his two siblings was the power of knowledge.

This meant that school fees were always prioritised in the Maharaj household and they were never burdened by student loans. Yuresh has always looked up to his well-read and articulate father, who had wanted to study law but as a young man did not have the funds to pursue this dream. His father's passion for history and mathematics led him to teaching and Ram retired as a high school principal. In retirement he joined a colleague to run an insurance brokerage firm in Durban, in so doing ending up in the same industry as his son.

Yuresh graduated with a degree in accounting in 1998 from what is today the University of KwaZulu-Natal and joined Deloitte in Durban a year later. After completing his articles, he joined the Deloitte office in Johannesburg in 2003 and was promoted to partner in the insurance audits division three years later. Insurance is an industry that always appealed to him as 'it is a noble principle to pool funds to give people the assurance that they will be taken care of when the unforeseen happens'.

Liberty's Yuresh Maharaj *(Photo: Michelle Nursey)*

He ended up spending a decade at Deloitte, progressing to head of insurance at the firm. In this role he was tasked with growing the practice and representing the South African arm at the regional platform for Europe, the Middle East and Africa.

In 2015, he decided it was time for a change. During his time at Deloitte he had been on the advisory side, telling businesses what to do but not having to implement any business decisions himself. For a long time, he had been curious about how it would be to work on the other side of the table. So, after ten years with the audit firm, he took the leap and joined Liberty – one of his clients – in August 2015 as an executive in group finance. Three years later, Yuresh was promoted to financial director.

205

IT'S NOT JUST ABOUT THE MONEY

'The ethos of this business has always resonated with me,' Yuresh says. 'Working in finance, it is easy to get lost in the numbers. But what's more important is the ability to fulfil promises to customers in moments when claims are high, such as now with the [COVID-19] pandemic. It's times like these that prove that job satisfaction goes beyond monetary rewards.'

The pandemic was a big blow for the insurance industry. Liberty Holdings posted a R1.5 billion loss in 2020, a big shock after a R3.2 billion profit the previous year. 'The financial impact was significant, but the impact we had on society made it all worth it,' Yuresh says. 'We are truly living out our purpose.'

He admits that the pandemic caught them by surprise to a great extent; no crisis simulation could have prepared them for its far-reaching effects. But it helped to have a strong team around him.

'We handled it in a phased approach, starting with ensuring the health and safety of our employees and advisers. In a matter of two weeks, we equipped everyone to work remotely. To date, 95% of our staff are working from home.'

He recounts proudly how they we were able to produce their financial reports on time, despite working remotely and virtually. 'We kept the finance function ticking over through a committee structure, having the right expertise to handle different facets such as the balance sheet and liquidity.'

Unexpectedly, Yuresh considers this experience to be one of the highlights of his career. He is thankful for the opportunity to provide financial leadership to a mammoth financial services company during trying times. It was a harrowing year, with claims increasing dramatically because of illness, death and job losses.

'The company was privy to some really heartbreaking stories that accompanied claims. And while we could have been led by business-minded instincts to find ways of reducing payouts, we did the right thing by finding ways to honour them instead.'

The coronavirus pandemic placed a great financial burden on Liberty, but it is not the first major crisis Yuresh has had to face as financial director.

At midnight on 14 June 2018, the company realised that their IT system had been hacked.

Yuresh was about to set off to London for an investor roadshow and was disheartened to be missing Father's Day that Sunday. Neither the work trip nor quality family time took place, as the executive team spent the weekend at the office trying to figure out how to respond to the attack and to ensure that all stakeholders were adequately informed about the incident.

'We were targeted as a financial services company, given how much personal information we hold,' Yuresh explains. 'But we kept calm and investigated the extent of the breach, with safeguarding our IT posture and data being our key priority. We continue to strengthen our IT infrastructure to ensure that customer information is protected.'

The takeaways from that experience include communicating honestly and regularly with stakeholders, engaging in rational and information-based decision-making, and taking appropriate measures to avoid it happening again in future.

Beyond managing crises, Yuresh's role requires active participation in strategy development. While he believes determining a vision is important to push the organisation forward, he warns against articulating everything to the nth degree and forgetting to take action. It's crucial to lay down building blocks and start implementing the vision.

'Analysis paralysis gets you nowhere. Rather go out and have the freedom to do what is necessary while retaining the ability to auto-correct. Allowing people to experiment is good, but it is also important to have checkpoints to review progress and consider changes.'

MOVING FORWARD

Liberty is more than 60 years old. It has amalgamated with many entities over the years, but each has come with its own way of doing things. When Yuresh became financial director, one of his first challenges was modernising the finance function while keeping the core infrastructure stable.

'Managing changes such as automating processes needs to be handled delicately because doing it too quickly can upset the functioning of the team. The human element is quite profound; we have close to 700 people in finance teams, across the continent, who need to be empowered. We have a finance modernisation programme that aims to turn our chief finance officers into chief value operators.'

Many of the team members Yuresh is referring to have significant institutional experience, having worked for the group for decades. The challenge is to help them change for the future without making them feel redundant. These changes include going on a journey to embrace technology and so reduce processing times by automating many functions.

Management has also embarked on entrenching a growth mindset among employees. For Yuresh, this includes having a learning day once a week for his finance staff, where they learn how to improve efficiencies in their roles and can stretch themselves beyond finance. He is particularly keen on people learning how the use of analytics can help speed up and simplify tasks, something Yuresh wishes he had spent more time on early on in his career.

If he could give 25-year-old self some advice based on what he knows now, it would be to never underestimate yourself. 'We all have a level of self-resistance or doubt in ourselves. We often lack that extra layer of confidence to convince us that what seems impossible can, in fact, be done. Personally, I think I could have pushed myself harder. When you achieve one milestone, it should encourage you to go for another.'

Yuresh points out that today's young professionals live in a different world from the one in which he was moulded. Careers are less defined than they were in the past. This calls for finance professionals to go beyond finance and consider what else they can learn. It is people with this mentality Yuresh looks for when recruiting for his team.

Professionals today also have the 'power of mobility', which makes it easy to venture past local experiences. At Deloitte, Yuresh had secondment opportunities to the Boston and Luxembourg offices of the firm. 'The experiences were enriching, not only from a work perspective but also from a cultural one. Spending time overseas is something I will encourage my two young daughters to do when the time comes.'

Another word of wisdom from Yuresh for young professionals is about kindness. The accounting profession promises good financial benefits, but that should not be the ultimate goal in pursuing this career, he says. 'Make sure your career path leads you towards an organisation whose values are aligned to yours. That is the most rewarding thing for both employer and employee, because when your values are in sync, you get the best out of the organisation and vice versa. It brings about a greater sense of accomplishment than a plump pay check.'

USING FACTS TO GROW

Given the assiduousness with which Yuresh responds to questions, he comes across as a limitless source of well-considered ideas. Autobiographies of inspirational leaders such as Barack Obama, Bill Gates and Richard Branson are some of his favourite books. He has gleaned many lessons from the way these icons have led.

Apart from autobiographies, he recommends the book *Factfulness: Ten Reasons We're Wrong About the World*, which encourages the 'stress-reducing habit of only carrying opinions for which you have strong supporting facts'.

Yuresh's management style is to follow a collaborative process where any ideas from his team backed up by facts are considered. 'I do my best to ensure that people have enough space to perform. Empowerment is critical for me. This includes being available to provide support to team members but without making them feel like you are stifling their efforts. I take part in mentoring, and it's really heart-warming to see individuals progress to senior positions.'

To get ahead in any corporation requires commitment and perseverance, he says. And you need to be in the habit of doing rather than talking. 'The accounting function is more than just closing the books; it's a hub that drives the strategy of the organisation. Individuals hoping to excel need to pass the value dimension test by demonstrating that they're strategy enablers and executors.'

Successful professionals are those who determine their purpose early on in their career and join organisations that are compatible with who they want to be. For Yuresh, finding a home at Liberty worked out perfectly, as it is 'morally and culturally aligned' to his desire to see South Africans be financially free.

Liberty was founded by Sir Donald Gordon, who, according to the company's website, 'watched his father work hard all his life yet reap little financial reward for his efforts. This struggle ignited in him the overwhelming belief that all people should have the opportunity to grow their wealth and leave a proud legacy for their family.'

Yuresh experienced the power of financial freedom on a very personal level when his father – who was exceptionally healthy and never had to set foot in a hospital – passed away in the winter of 2020 due to COVID-19. It was a devastating blow to Yuresh, who considers his father his hero.

His father had always been a firm believer in insurance and took out cover for various eventualities in life. Witnessing the benefits of insurance in his father's life has reaffirmed to Yuresh that he is in the right industry, the right company and the right job.

RONEL VAN DIJK

From waitress to restaurateur

— INTERVIEW: MARCH 2021 —

As a young accounting student at Stellenbosch University, Ronel van Dijk waited tables for pocket money at the popular Spur restaurant in her hometown, Parow. Ronel was a top achiever at school and was fortunate to have a bursary from the Yvonne Parfitt Bursary Trust that paid for her tuition and books. But she still needed to cover her pocket money and transport from Parow to Stellenbosch, and that's where the Spur came in.

Twelve years after that student job, the tables were turned when she was appointed financial director at the Spur Corporation. And still her connection with Spur continues – today she's an investor in a company that owns four of the group's restaurants.

She remembers her time as a waitress fondly. 'Waiting tables teaches you many skills: multitasking, timekeeping, handling feedback, customer relations, and giving and taking instructions. I became quite good at it and I had great relationships with some of the regulars. One couple actually invited me to their daughter's wedding!'

Having grown up in Parow and having had a very Afrikaans upbringing, Ronel jokes about how waiting tables also forced her to improve her spoken English.

After completing her honours degree at Stellenbosch in 1994, Ronel joined Arthur Andersen for a three-year training contract. On completion, she spent a year at the Arthur Andersen office in London before returning to South Africa in 1999 to become a manager at the firm.

In due course, her career experienced a serendipitous encounter when Spur became one of her audit clients.

STAYING TRUE TO YOURSELF

In 2001, the Enron scandal broke. The corporation collapsed after allegations of fraudulent financial reporting, resulting in the biggest bankruptcy case in US history. In 2002, Arthur Andersen, which had been auditing the company for over 16 years, was found guilty of aiding and abetting the Enron fraud, which in turn led to the collapse of this global Big Five auditing firm.

KPMG took over most of Arthur Andersen's clients and employees, but Ronel soon decided KPMG was not for her. 'The culture at the firm was quite different. People observed strict start and end times each day and there was a real hierarchy of authority that I was not used to. At Arthur Andersen we had a culture of working hard and playing hard. We worked long hours, but when we had a celebration, we had real fun.'

After she resigned, Spur offered her a position as a financial manager. The group operates on a franchising model, which means that they do not own any restaurants but earn a franchise fee from their franchisees. When Ronel joined the company, the two main restaurant brands were Spur Steak Ranches and Panarottis, a pizza/pasta chain.

'Spur has been very meaningful in my life; if it hadn't been for the money I earned as a waitress I would not have been able to afford the transport to and from university. When I joined the head office, the company was changing from a big–small company to a small–big company and my role focused on ensuring that the control environment was formalised and improved, and compliance and regulatory processes were in place.'

Ronel was responsible for the finance function, given that the financial director, Dean Hyde, was more involved in laying down the commercial direction of the company. 'I was promoted to the role of FD [financial director] in 2006, following Dean's resignation a year earlier. I consider myself lucky; I was at the right place at the right time.

PPC's Ronel van Dijk *(Photo: Stella Sassen)*

It was a great opportunity for me to grow given that I was relatively inexperienced.'

In the early stages of Ronel's career as financial director, the group embarked on an expansion drive, increasing the number of their restaurants by over 10%, eventually having 333 outlets, including some in the UK, Australia and parts of Africa.

'Other than managing the finance function in different jurisdictions, the biggest challenge was changing mindsets of management and restaurateurs. "You are as good as your last meal and your customer will not wait," was the mantra they lived by. Although being focused on the customer is a good thing, an organisation should not circumvent proper internal controls and good corporate governance.'

In March 2002, the King II Report on Corporate Governance was published, recommending the implementation of a philosophy pillared on leadership, sustainability and good corporate citizenship.

'I think all companies go through a phase in their life cycle when they need to put structures and processes in place as they become bigger. When I joined, a certain maturity was required of the company. Implementing change is not easy; you end up having a lot of heated debates with your stakeholders.'

If you want to implement change, you need resilience and perseverance, Ronel says. 'You have to keep insisting that things be done a certain way and eventually the penny will drop. You also need to demonstrate *why* the change is being made; people must be convinced that it's necessary for their own good before they will accept it.'

ON BEING THE ONLY WOMAN IN THE BOARDROOM

When Ronel was appointed to the Spur Corporation's board, she was the only woman among the ten directors. During her career, she's faced a number of challenges because of her gender.

'You often find that there are men who have their opinion about women and where they belong. They would speak among themselves in a manner that didn't recognise that there was a lady in the room, which made me uncomfortable, particularly because I was quite young and not so confident in myself.'

While much still remains to be done in terms of gender diversity in corporate South Africa, the Spur Corporation appointed Val Nichas and Cristina Teixeira to the roles of CEO and CFO, respectively, in 2021.

With more and more women taking up leadership positions in the corporate arena, I ask Ronel what advice she has for them. 'I think they should stand their ground and take the punches that come their way. Even though men and women often act in the same way, they are unfortunately judged by different sets of rules. When a man gets angry and bangs the table, he is seen as assertive. When a woman does the same thing, she is considered emotional.'

She admits to losing her temper on occasion. 'But I'm humble enough to apologise when I'm in the wrong.'

Ronel advises women to stay true to themselves and not try to be 'one of the boys'. 'I don't think it's necessary for women to do things they don't enjoy. For instance, in the corporate environment, you find that companies often favour activities that naturally exclude women, like golf days and booking corporate boxes at sports stadiums. Despite being an avid sports fan, I often wasn't invited to stadium games, because it was assumed that I wouldn't enjoy them. Women should speak up and push for things that are more inclusive, rather than spending long hours engaged in activities they don't enjoy just so that they can be part of the clique.'

Female managers should also stand their ground when things are said that they find inappropriate. 'Often you find that people will appreciate being corrected. They may not have meant to be offensive and raising the issue helps to educate them on more fitting behaviour. Although the topic is an emotional one, there are unemotional ways of bringing the discussion up, so it is also important to develop your communication skills.'

By the time Ronel left the Spur Corporation (in March 2018), the turnover of the group had more than tripled, going from R200 million to R670 million during her time as CFO. The combined revenue of the franchised stores had increased from R2.2 billion in 2006 to R7.2 billion in 2018. The group had also expanded its restaurant brands to include John Dory's Fish & Grill, Captain Dorego's, The Hussar Grill, RocoMamas and Casa Bella.

And what better testament to the group's favourable outlook could there be than Ronel herself recently investing in four of the group's franchised restaurants?

Ronel has gone from strength to strength. In July 2018, she was appointed a non-executive director of Grand Parade Investments, a group that has investments in various casinos and 91% ownership of Burger King South Africa, and in June 2019 joined the board of Adcorp Holdings. Adcorp is a listed workplace solutions company, with over 45 000 employees in South Africa and Australia.

Outside of the corporate world, she also makes time for outreach activities. Ronel is a founding member of the Western Cape Development Board of the Early Care Foundation. The foundation aims to teach women to run their own small businesses, to empower them to teach young children and to change the trajectory for children in low-income areas.

Ronel's interest in uplifting children from disadvantaged backgrounds stretches back to Mandela Day 2012, when she launched the Spur Foundation and chaired its first Board of Trustees. It was established with a donation of R670 000 from the Spur Corporation, resonating with the '67 minutes' theme of Mandela Day, and is known today for its 'Full Tummy Fund', which runs educational and nutritional programmes for children from less fortunate neighbourhoods.

A LEARNING CURVE AT PPC

In October 2019, Ronel was approached to serve as interim CFO at the cement company PPC after both the CEO and 'second in command' executive had left the company in quick succession. It was like jumping into a fire.

During this time she was responsible for putting out financial statements. 'Soon after I started, we also began a programme to restructure the group because it was overleveraged, particularly with respect to debt in the DRC [Democratic Republic of Congo], which had recourse to the South African business.'

While the board was still dealing with this problem, the COVID-19 pandemic hit. The audit of the 31 March 2020 financial statements was conducted under unusual circumstances, with both internal accounting and external audit staff working from home.

'It was terrible timing, because I didn't know the company that well, having joined only months before. Yet I had to manage the process from home in Cape Town, with the head office being in Johannesburg. We also could not perform stock counts at year-end on 31 March, because the lockdown had begun five days before.'

It was a stressful time, with the audit eventually taking three months longer than usual to complete and an increased level of scrutiny from the auditors. Thankfully the company was given special dispensation by the Johannesburg Stock Exchange to report their results a week late.

'An additional challenge was the intense negotiations with the banks for our finance arrangements, with vast amounts of information having to be prepared for submission. The level of uncertainty meant that we had to have a very detailed "going concern" note in our annual financial statements.'

Ronel has a level-headed approach to unexpected events that you have no control over, such as the COVID-19 pandemic. 'All you can do is make the best of the situation and go with the flow. I've been fortunate to have had great support from PPC's CEO, Roland van Wijnen. He is always realistic about a situation, often saying, "It is what it is." You can't change what happened, but you can change what you do about it.'

Even though her stint as CFO of PPC has been the most demanding time in her career so far, she is grateful for it. 'It's in difficult times that you learn the most, because when things are easy, you don't learn anything new,' she says. 'I learnt a lot about people and a lot about myself. I learnt that I have more patience than I thought, as well as perseverance. It's possible to gather the troops and get things done in a virtual environment, and I realised, in general, the human race is very adaptable. Most people are committed and loyal and they appreciate recognition and gratitude.'

She encourages young professionals to read well and widely, particularly on leadership skills, mindfulness and philosophy. 'This kind of literature has been quite beneficial for me during my time at PPC. I will be honest: it was very difficult. But I've learnt a lot, I've met really wonderful people and I've done things in business that I would not have done otherwise. I told the finance team at PPC the other day that I will not pretend I enjoyed it, but it was an honour to serve them as CFO and to make a contribution to a company that is 129 years old and whose existence was under threat. I believe I've left it in a better condition than I found it.'

The uncertainty around the group led to the share price declining to less than 50 cents in November 2020. The price rose steadily after that, and at the time of our interview in March 2021 it was sitting at around R3. What part does she think she played in steadying the ship?

'As CFOs we don't like talking about ourselves, but I would say I feel like I stepped up to the plate when the company needed me. I sacrificed a lot of my time, including commuting from Cape Town to Johannesburg often. Despite my contract coming to an end, I stayed on because we had not found a replacement. It would have been easy to just resign and return to my semi-retired life, but loyalty is an important thing for me, and I wouldn't have slept well knowing I abandoned the company in its hour of need.'

She also feels she contributed to the lives of the people she worked with by teaching them about leadership and camaraderie in the workplace, introducing weekly training sessions that covered technical matters, software training and people skills, and by being available to the team when they need her.

Ronel's term at PPC ended in March 2021. A highlight of her time at the company was when they finally managed to remove the contingent obligation to PPC Barnet in the DRC by entering into a binding agreement with its lenders, terminating their right to recourse to PPC in South Africa. 'That untied PPC from a potential liability of US$175 million, which we expect will restore investor confidence and free management to focus on core operations.'

FINDING A SUCCESSFUL STRATEGY

When we start talking about the importance of strategy, she takes some time to consider the meaning of the word.

'A strategy is something that needs to be embedded into the organisation at every level, not just at management. It requires support of each person in the business who will play a part in its implementation. And also, you need moments of reflection along the way; it should be measurable. Are you still going where you thought you wanted to go, or do you need to change direction?'

She also points out that for a strategy to be successful, it has to be realistic and simple to understand. 'Everyone in the company should know what the strategy is and where they fit into its bigger picture. Without that you might as well not even start.'

Communication is as important in getting a strategy executed as it is in managing people, she says. 'I aspire to meet deadlines and to deliver on time every time, and it's a big thing for me that people communicate when they think they won't be able to deliver on time. If you don't tell me that you won't be able to do something by a certain time and I rely on you, then chances are that I won't be able to deliver, as I will be unable to help you meet the deadline. And if you don't tell me that you don't know how to do something, I won't know how to provide you with the relevant support. That is the essence of teamwork, isn't it?' she muses.

She does not believe in a strict hierarchy when it comes to management. 'My door is always open, and I think I have a collaborative leadership style. I welcome different opinions and I'm not shy to change my mind when convinced that a better idea has been presented.'

Ronel believes that having the support of your boss and giving support to your team are extremely important. 'Little things like checking in every day to find out how people are doing and what you can do to make their work easier make a world of difference. You learn how much people can cope with and how much they can get done. Furthermore, you get to treasure loyalty and commitment from those willing to stand with you through difficult times.'

Empowering her staff is also important to Ronel. 'I'm not the type of person who observes a strict hierarchy. I'm happy to put the person who prepared the document in front of the audience – be it Exco, the CEO or the board. That gives them exposure, grows them and teaches them.'

Our interview leaves me with the impression of someone with a people-centred management style. It is easy to understand why times when she receives thanks from those reporting to her count as major personal career highlights. 'It is extremely rewarding when I can make a difference in someone's life and contribute to their personal and professional growth. That is, after all, the main goal I strive for as a leader.'

NTOBEKO NYAWO

The chief truth officer

— INTERVIEW: JULY 2021 —

As a young boy in Mtubatuba in Zululand (now part of KwaZulu-Natal), Ntobeko Nyawo and his siblings were entrusted with his grandfather's large herd of Nguni cattle. When they were not in school, they had to find the greenest pastures among the misty hills. Looking back on his childhood today, Ntobeko has realised two things: first, his hometown is one of the most beautiful places on Earth, and secondly, looking after cattle planted the seed for a career in accounting and investing.

The cattle were not his property, but he had been given the responsibility of taking care of them, making sure that he found the best available meadow that would nurture them. And at the end of the day, he had to bring back as many head of cattle as he had gone out with, not a single one less. In Ntobeko's mind, this mirrors the duty of accountability and stewardship that accountants have, particularly those in financial services.

'I think it boils down to staying true,' Ntobeko explains. 'I think of the CFO as the chief truth officer in the organisation, who needs to be the central point of veracity about where we have come from, where we are and where we're headed. When I came back home and my grandfather asked me about the cattle, I had to truthfully report on what kind of day they had had and my thoughts on how we could better care for them.'

Redefine's Ntobeko Nyawo *(Photo: Redefine Properties)*

Ntobeko's matric results from Mlokothwa High School earned him a bursary from the De Beers Group to pursue an accounting degree at the then University of Natal. He graduated with a Bachelor of Commerce (Honours) degree in 2002 and joined De Beers in Johannesburg the following year. This was the first year the South African Institute of Chartered Accountants allowed article clerks to receive their mandatory three-year training through companies that were not audit firms.

ALEXANDER FORBES

As De Beers is the world's leading diamond company, Ntobeko's work was focused on mining finance. He fondly remembers Rocco Barnard, an engineer who taught him much about the business of mining. He found it interesting but not sufficiently captivating for a long-term career. Instead, he wanted to spread his wings to the world of investment finance, and when he learnt about a vacancy in an accounting role at Alexander Forbes, he submitted his CV.

Ntobeko was appointed head of BEE Consulting Services at Alexander Forbes in September 2006, where he was fortunate to work with mentors who nurtured him. A year later, he was appointed CFO of Alexander Forbes Emerging Markets, a division tasked with expanding this financial services group's footprint in Africa.

Many of Alexander Forbes' South African clients were setting up shop in other African countries, which meant making Alexander Forbes products and services available to serve them in those markets. This involved understanding the local business environment, complying with legislation, partnering with the right people and implementing appropriate technology to make the service line viable.

Ntobeko got to work alongside Geoffrey Nzau, at the time CEO of this 'unloved' division. The two of them worked hard to turn its cash flow problems around, with Ntobeko serving as CFO for close to two years and as COO from May 2009 to April 2011.

When the business was sold to the Marsh Group, he had to choose between remaining with Alexander Forbes and moving to Marsh. He stayed and assumed the role of financial director at Alexander Forbes Investments (AFI).

'It was at AFI that I really fell in love with investments,' Ntobeko says. 'Once again, I served first as CFO and then COO at this company, working with Derrick Msibi as CEO. We did amazing work during my six and a half years there, doubling the portfolio of assets under management from approximatelyR300 billion.'

One of the most difficult moments in Ntobeko's career was at AFI when the group was slapped with a massive tax bill by the South African Revenue Service. As CFO, Ntobeko had to present the merits of their defence to the taxman. If the assessment stood, it would have threatened the very existence of the company, but he successfully defended the company's position. He laughs when I point out that Edward Kieswetter, who was the group CEO of Alexander Forbes at the time, is now the tax service's commissioner. Talk about a small world!

TRANSITION TO REDEFINING PROPERTY INVESTMENTS

After a decade at Alexander Forbes, it was time for a change. Derrick Msibi took up the position of CEO at Stanlib and Ntobeko followed him there in June 2018, taking up the role of COO. Similar to his role at AFI, it again involved him with the leadership and management of an entity that invests money into different asset classes.

He found listed properties particularly interesting. So when the opportunity came to join South Africa's second largest real estate investment trust, he seized it without hesitation – the first step towards becoming the CFO of Redefine Properties (which happened in February 2021).

'This is a different and perhaps slightly more difficult challenge, because at an investment company such as Stanlib or AFI, you pick what counters to allocate money to. At Redefine, I'm charged with running the counter itself. I joined the company during the [COVID-19] pandemic, a time when the entire property industry is under immense strain. If I manage to contribute and help turn the business around, it will be a significant professional achievement.'

Some of Ntobeko's friends think he is crazy to venture into a property company at such a volatile time. But he believes leaders should not be judged on how well they run businesses during good times, but rather on 'how well they adapt during tough times'.

The Redefine management is aware that certain shifts in the industry were not necessarily caused by the coronavirus crisis but rather accelerated by it. This calls for extra effort to adapt to emerging trends, such as hybrid work models where many companies have some employees working from the office while others work remotely.

Another aspect that was being considered even before the pandemic was reducing the company's debt. At the mid-year presentation to investors in 2020, Ntobeko's team were already able to announce reducing the loan-to-value ratio by about 4%. Maintaining that trend will not be easy, though, given strained cash flows resulting from declining rental incomes and increased vacancies caused by the pandemic.

'I'm an eternal optimist. Everything that has been thrown at humanity we've managed to overcome. That's why I was unperturbed by the idea of joining Redefine at this time, because I'm in it for the long haul. And our approach to the pandemic mirrors this attitude; we gave tenants relief because we want to support them to survive the downturn.'

During 2020, Redefine and other real estate investment trusts gave their tenants over R3 billion relief in the form of reduced rental rates and extended payment terms. While they realise this may be destructive to their profit margins in the short term, Ntobeko is of the opinion that it will be value accretive in the long term. It will help to keep tenants in business and allow Redefine to retain customers in their properties in future.

This has been particularly necessary for enterprises that were not allowed to trade during certain levels of the government's enforced lockdown. The recovery in the retail sector has been much better than in commercial spaces, while growth in the logistics and industrial sector has been fast-tracked by widespread acceptance of e-commerce during the pandemic.

A major macroeconomic challenge Ntobeko had to face in his first seven months as CFO of Redefine was the outbreak of violence in parts of KwaZulu-Natal and Gauteng, during which many retail centres were looted and damaged. Out of a portfolio of over R75 billion, the affected sites fortunately represented only 2% of Redefine's properties. They have since submitted insurance claims and begun the process of rebuilding in affected areas.

STRATEGY AND LEADERSHIP LESSONS

'Strategy is about connecting the dots to transform the client experience. What should shape your business is the evolution of your clients. I know there are other things a business needs to think about, like compliance, but I've never seen a successful business being built on the back of how well it masters regulation. At the end of the day, it's all about your clients.'

Ntobeko admires a company that provides a very simple product but has a service offering that keeps them ahead of their competitors. He mentions Starbucks as an example: they sell coffee, but the way they serve it is what sets them apart. Anyone can source the excellent coffee beans, but not everyone can replicate the overall customer experience.

'In the listed-property space, we're focusing on transforming the customer experience by adapting to trends such as hybrid work spaces and using technology to augment human potential. For example, our almost 4 500 tenants are able to open an online platform and view their billing status at any time, without waiting for us to send them a statement.'

To execute a strategy effectively, it helps if you are working with people that you like. In this regard, Ntobeko enjoys working with Andrew König (CEO) and Leon Kok (COO), who he thinks have the right mentality to 're-imagine the real estate investment trust of the future'.

Apart from client-centricity, the economics of a strategy are also very important. For example, property investment trusts rely on debt to fund identified opportunities, but the gearing needs to be balanced to manage the overall balance sheet strength and the liquidity profile. Sustainability is also critical; if you have a client focus and the right economics but you damage the planet in implementing the strategy, you will lose out in the long term as corrective action will be expensive.

When it comes to hiring and promoting staff, Ntobeko thinks diversity is imperative. To him, diversity means including people not only from different cultural backgrounds but also from different fields, as they can bring new ways of thinking to a team. He explains that accountants, for example, are very task oriented and therefore a management team made up only of people with an accounting background would struggle to excel in a world where using data differentiates the winners from the losers.

'We are grappling with how we can make Redefine a suitable environment for data scientists or people with other diversified skill sets to enhance our core property competencies. We also look for people who like what they do and have a passion for learning. Our environment is changing rapidly. We can't continue to do things in the same way we've always done. Learning new things, unlearning old things and adapting to a fluid landscape are what will help us thrive.'

Ntobeko's management and leadership style is to play each individual to their strengths, helping them to find their sweet spot and perform at their best. While it is inevitable that there will be conflict among individuals on a team, he believes that if team members are encouraged to act in a mature way, it is possible to zoom in on the real issues at play and deal with them.

LEARN, CHANGE AND READ

Ntobeko's does his best to live up to the meaning of his name – humble – and he sees himself as a servant rather than a boss. Apart from teaching him a sense of responsibility for the possessions of others, Ntobeko's grandfather also taught him to be transparent in everything he does and that there is no substitute for hard work. You might be talented, but to be successful in life, you need to combine what nature has given you with a good work ethic, he believes.

If Ntobeko could go back to the start of his career and do things over, he would have liked to become an investment professional sooner. He is convinced that people who enjoy what they do are usually also very good at it. If you can figure it out early enough, you will have enough time to become an expert in what you are passionate about.

To him, the ability to learn, the capacity to change and the willingness to use different skills are pivotal to becoming a well-rounded professional. Ntobeko advises young professionals to learn as much as they can about the things that make the modern world tick, such as technology.

'We all have our purpose in this life, and it is essential for you to be yourself,' he advises. 'Successful nations are those that are made up of citizens who know what role they are best suited for in their society. That said, we should also have fun! No one has ever managed to escape death, so best we find ways to enjoy life while we still have it.'

Ntobeko subscribes to the maxim that 'good leaders are good readers'. He recommends *Good to Great: Why Some Companies Make the Leap ... and Others Don't* by Jim Collins for insight into what makes a company work, while Steve Jobs' biography is important for revealing how Apple became an authority in meeting customer needs. Ntobeko has even contributed to the book *Building Capital*, written by a former colleague at AFI, Muitheri Wahome, a worthwhile read about the history of asset management in South Africa.

Given how often Ntobeko mentioned the customer in our discussion, it is clear that this chief truth officer is focused on redefining the listed-property space to become a place that will benefit both company and client.

PIETER VAN DER WESTHUIZEN

The toughest year ever

— INTERVIEW: MAY 2021 —

For Pieter van der Westhuizen there are distinct similarities between the worlds of accounting and medicine, perhaps explaining why he has worked in the medical environment ever since he qualified as a chartered accountant in 1996.

'I've been with the same company for many years because I quite like the clinical environment. It's very regulated; the nurses with their stripes on their uniforms are like military personnel. In medicine there's a lot of discipline and you have to stick to rules, which is similar to the accounting profession, where we have standards that we must abide by.'

Pieter exhibits a calm and attentive personality, taking time to learn about his interviewer despite having just returned from leave and having a crazy schedule to attend to. It was most probably this same calm that helped him through a major crisis in June 2020, in the midst of the COVID-19 pandemic. CEO Shrey Viranna had resigned in January of that year and Pieter served as acting CEO for several months before Peter Wharton-Hood took over the role in September.

On Monday, 8 June, Pieter got up at 5 am as usual and opened his emails to see what would be on his plate that week. What he saw was the ultimate definition of all hell breaking loose. The company's IT system, which supports 66 hospitals in South Africa, had been hacked.

Life Healthcare's Pieter van der Westhuizen *(Photo: Marinda van Zyl)*

'It was a very stressful time. The attack took a toll on me personally, because the repercussions of such attacks on a hospital chain can make the difference between whether somebody lives or dies. It is disheartening that there are people in this world who would put other people's lives at risk to secure a ransom.'

The company acted immediately and took systems offline in an attempt to actively contain the attack. External cyber security experts and forensic teams were brought on board to advise and supplement internal teams and capacity.

In line with business continuity plans, hospitals and administrative offices switched over to backup manual processing systems and continued to function, albeit with some administrative delays. The security incident affected admissions systems, business processing systems and email servers.

As acting CEO, Pieter issued a statement assuring communities that the criminal attack would not affect the quality of patient care. He lamented that something like this had occurred at a time when their facilities were working hard to fight the COVID-19 pandemic.

For a month, Life operated manually, experiencing delays in completing patient billing, submitting claims to medical aids, processing supplier invoices and producing financial results. By early July, the group had restored its IT systems and was able to operate normally in all material respects.

'Our training as chartered accountants helps us to handle crises such as this. Your studies require you to be meticulous; you need to plan things and approach them step by step. I always write down everything. Even if I never refer back to it, the process helps a lot, because the simple act of writing enhances your memory.'

To Pieter preparation reduces stress. 'There's nothing worse than going into a meeting unprepared'.

LANDMARK TRANSACTIONS

It was the toughest year of his career so far, says Pieter about 2020. Not only did he have to step into the demanding role of chief executive temporarily, but he also had to deal with the COVID-19 pandemic while preserving the company purse as CFO.

Thankfully purse preservation runs in the family, with Pieter's father having been a bank manager in his day. 'My dad actually inspired me to become an accountant. I admired how he used to wear a suit and tie every day and looked very professional,' Pieter recalls. 'During the holidays, he used to rope in my brother and me to work in the bank, which further gave me a feel for numbers. When the time came to make subject choices at my school, I found accounting to be a natural choice.'

Pieter obtained his accounting degree from the University of Pretoria in 1993 and joined Coopers & Lybrand for his articles a year later. He completed his training contract in 1996 and joined President Medical Investments (Presmed) in 1999, which later became part of Afrox Healthcare.

His various roles in the finance department at Afrox included assisting in the delisting from the Johannesburg Stock Exchange (JSE) in 2005 and its subsequent relisting as Life Healthcare in 2010. He was appointed group CFO in 2013.

Pieter has worked with a number of the company staff for decades, ever since he was an article clerk on the Presmed audit, and he appreciates the culture of the company built by a great group of people.

And, he says, not one day is the same at Life Healthcare. 'There are different deadlines to meet, which keep you on your toes. There hasn't been a single year when I've looked back and felt like it was a boring or unfulfilling year. I've been involved in the kind of transactions many chartered accountants only dream of experiencing.'

The transactions Pieter refers to include Life Healthcare's listing on the JSE and raising US$680 billion through one of Africa's largest ever initial public offerings.

'Listing a company takes long hours because you have to go through a tedious process of ensuring that you meet extensive listing requirements. It involves preparing mountains of documentation and working with different stakeholders.'

Another landmark transaction was the rights offer in 2016 to acquire the UK Alliance Medical Group for R14.2 billion, a company described as 'Europe's leading independent provider of imaging services'.

'This transaction happened after we had gone through an extensive search internationally to identify a company that fitted our strategy of incorporating an imaging service provider into our stable. We then had to go through a competitive bid process, which involves applying profound judgement and negotiation to ensure that the price is right.'

Getting the deal over the line is a fulfilling experience, but the work is not done yet; the next step is to integrate the company into the group, which requires conscientious leadership for functions such as finance.

Prior to the acquisition of Alliance, Pieter was involved in the acquisition of 81% of the Polish hospital business Scanmed Multimedis for R427 million. The group disposed of this investment in 2020 for R1.29 billion, after deciding to focus on growing their non-acute earnings.

STRATEGY AND DEALING WITH COVID-19

Life Healthcare's vision is to be a global, people-centred, diversified healthcare organisation. The group's strategy is to offer an integrated healthcare model by focusing on clinical excellence and the use of analytics and technology.

Asked what strategy means to Life, Pieter says that it is all about how you get to your vision. 'You need to adapt your strategy regularly. We have a longer-term view, looking 20 years ahead to project what the healthcare industry might look like, and then we play it back and put business plans in place that will deliver what we forecast. In doing that, you need to be careful not to go into too much detail too soon, because that opens the door to finding reasons why you can't deliver rather than focusing on what you need to do to deliver.'

Despite a topsy-turvy year, the half-year financial report in March 2021 showed that the group remained profitable and saw a 4% growth in revenue from continuing operations. As a group of hospitals, the company had to confront the disease on its own doorstep: it affected more than 3 000 employees and claimed the lives of more than 20.

The leadership of the company donated a portion of their salaries to funds established to benefit employees and contractors. Approximately R6 million was paid to over 1 500 employees and those who could not isolate or quarantine – more than 800 – were provided with company-funded accommodation.

In the company's latest integrated report, management note that despite doing a lot right, there are a number of things they could have done differently. These lessons are being documented in a handbook for responding to infectious epidemics in future and include responses such as reconsidering short-term retention schemes, educating staff on preventing transmission, better psychosocial support and having a national service level agreement with government.

From a financial perspective, fewer general hospital admissions for non-COVID-19 infections and elective surgeries threatened the company's stability, and they consequently implemented measures such as suspending dividends, amending borrowing arrangements, reviewing supplier terms and delaying capital projects to weather the storm.

ADVICE FOR YOUNG PROFESSIONALS

Despite his success today, Pieter believes there are things he could have done differently in the past. For one, he wishes he had taken the opportunity to travel internationally when he had secondment opportunities. 'Experiencing a different culture and environment is invaluable; I've seen that in the course of our international acquisitions. It's a good thing to expose yourself early, because when you are older you're more entrenched in your local way of thinking.'

'I should also have worked harder in school,' he exclaims. 'I think I was a bit lucky, because I don't recall putting in my best effort in exams. And I should have studied a more broadly, not focusing just on accounting subjects but also taking social science disciplines to broaden my knowledge base.'

Finally, he bemoans never learning a foreign language. 'My wife is of Austrian descent and speaks fluent German. She would have been delighted if I had taken the time to learn *Deutsch*.'

After a taxing day at the office, Pieter finds that exercise and spending time with his family help him recharge. So he tries to get home before dinner time at least three days a week and goes on an intense morning jog as regularly.

For the past 20 years, the Van der Westhuizen family have been happy residents of Tshwane, even if it means Pieter has to make a 40-kilometre commute to the office in Johannesburg every day. His better half could not contemplate leaving the silent capital, and Pieter lives by the dictum 'happy wife, happy life'.

'I once almost convinced her,' he says. 'After seven years of me working in Joburg, she agreed to sell the house and make the move. We got a really good offer for the property. We signed and I celebrated because I thought my long trips had come to an end. The following morning, she had changed her mind!'

RIAAN KOPPESCHAAR

Diversity's advocate

— INTERVIEW: MAY 2021 —

When I first heard Riaan Koppeschaar's surname, I couldn't help but think of the Swahili verb *kopesha,* which means 'lend'. That his surname should sound like the word for generating debt in the most widely spoken indigenous language on the African continent is quite ironic, because as group financial director at the mining company Exxaro, Riaan is quite averse to undue borrowing.

In fact, Riaan takes pride in the fact that the founding shareholders have settled the acquisition debt used to create Exxaro, one of the top coal producers and the largest black-owned company in South Africa.

Exxaro came into being in November 2006. At the time, Riaan was the general manager of corporate finance and treasury at Kumba Resources. Kumba's coal division merged with Eyesizwe Coal, creating Exxaro, and Riaan continued in the same role at the new company. He was appointed to the executive team in June 2016.

Even a cursory glance at Riaan's CV will show you that he has always been a top performer. He 'never battled with academics' and received both his undergraduate and honours degrees in accounting cum laude at the University of Pretoria.

After completing his articles at Coopers & Lybrand in 1997, he joined Iscor, which unbundled its mining assets into Kumba Resources in 2001.

'Since completing my articles, I've essentially been with the same company, and for the most part in the treasury and corporate finance division,' he says. 'I find treasury interesting, as managing exposure can be quite a rewarding process when you get it right. Because of the financial risks in mining, you can't afford to have a liquidity crisis because of having taken on a lot of debt but having insufficient cash inflows to make payments on time.'

Beyond liquidity risks, the treasury function is also tasked with managing foreign exchange exposure, as sales and certain purchases are made in foreign currency and therefore financial performance is impacted by movements in the exchange rate. The treasury function manages this risk by entering into different financial instruments, such as foreign exchange contracts. Riaan also branched out into the corporate finance space, overseeing Exxaro's investment and capital allocation processes.

He adds that although the mining sector is affected by commodity prices, these are largely beyond the control of the finance function. 'We are a cyclical industry where timing is everything. You need to invest at the bottom of the cycle when prices are low, and sell at the top when prices are high.'

FINANCIAL ACHIEVEMENTS

In Riaan's first full year as financial director, Exxaro's earnings before interest, tax, depreciation and amortisation (EBITDA) increased from R6 billion to R7.2 billion. In 2018, the performance remained stable, but in 2019 it fell sharply – to R5.8 billion – because of low export prices for coal, the group's primary business.

'While Exxaro's operations were declared an essential service during the [COVID-19] lockdown period, and able to operate, the environment remained challenging,' Riaan writes in his overview for the 2020 financial year. 'However, our managed operations were able to show strength and resilience, resulting in a 25% increase in core EBITDA to R7.3 billion.'

Although financial performance was buoyed by commodity prices and government support, technology also had a significant part in the success of 2020. The company increasingly used drones to obtain images

Exxaro's Riaan Koppeschaar *(Photo: Neil Weideman)*

for planning and executing the mining process. Riaan's finance team similarly had to adapt to the virtual environment for their various operations, including adopting cloud-based accounting systems. That they were able to provide audited reports on time with both the finance team and the auditors working virtually is something Riaan sees as a major achievement.

TEAM-PLAYER LEADERSHIP

This feat was the result of Riaan's 'team-player' leadership style. He strongly believes that 'no single person is an expert' and ever since his appointment as financial director he has emphasised the importance of teamwork. He relies heavily on his team and ensures that oversight does not turn into micromanagement.

'When I give a project to someone, I let them run with it. It's their responsibility to ensure it is executed properly, as they will be accountable for the outcome. However, I let them know that my door is wide open if they need input or guidance. That is what I believe is true empowerment; it makes all the difference between being a leader and being a manager.'

Riaan learnt some of his leadership skills while completing the Advanced Management Programme at the INSEAD Business School in France. The programme is designed for senior executives, primarily those at director level, and involves doing course work and case studies to gain new insights and broaden their perspectives to a global level.

An important lesson to him was about the need for diversity in a team. Team members should have different skill sets and come from different cultural backgrounds, which they can merge and distil into efficiency. This perspective is backed by research showing that workplace diversity contributes to higher productivity.

Riaan looks for three elements when selecting and promoting team members. 'First is capability. The employee would need to have the requisite technical skills to perform their job,' he explains. 'Second, they need to demonstrate that they are willing to put in the effort that is required for the team to achieve its objectives. Finally, they need to have the desired impact, because even if you can complete the work, the eventual impact of your work may be contrary to the organisation's culture and values.'

With 150 people reporting to him, whether directly or indirectly, Riaan often has to navigate a number of human resource issues, including keeping staff motivated and creating growth opportunities. 'Ultimately what makes the company work is its people. It is a delicate balancing act, because if people think their voices are not heard, they feel unimportant, and their performance levels drop. As a board, we are constantly looking for opportunities to progress our staff.

'On the other hand, leadership also calls for honesty, and occasionally you have to tell someone that they're not suited for the role they were hoping to get and that they need to reconsider their options.'

CRISIS MANAGEMENT AND STRATEGY

The mining industry is fraught with crises. Concerns include inconsistent demand, environmental destruction and worker safety. As a result, mining businesses invest heavily in risk management programmes and senior management have to focus on risk containment.

'This is the advantage I think our industry has over many others when faced with something like COVID-19,' Riaan says. 'It's important not to overreact, but to think through problems rationally and then take action. The stock market is a good example of how crises present us with opportunities. If you bought shares at this time last year, you would be smiling all the way to the bank today with shares gaining over 30% in the period.'

Riaan's role also requires him to participate in developing the company's strategy. 'Strategy is all about foresight,' he explains. 'You need to keep an eye on the way the world is moving and align yourself to the trends. Climate change has been a hot topic for over a decade now and therefore those who invest in cleaner technologies will position themselves to benefit from the trend. In developing a long-term strategy, you need to determine what will be considered problems in future and develop capabilities to provide solutions.'

In this regard, Exxaro strives to be an active participant in the transition to a low-carbon economy by investing in renewable energy. In

Riaan the company has an experienced and loyal steward to man its financial levers in its quest for carbon neutrality.

ADVICE FOR PROFESSIONALS

If he had to start his career over again, Riaan says he would choose a different path. He has a great interest in deal making and would pursue becoming an investment management professional. He says he doesn't have enough time to read widely, but he does cast his eyes on the *Wall Street Journal,* the American daily focused on international financial markets, when he can.

Riaan is very aware that times have changed for professionals and he believes they are unlikely to have only a single career during their lifetimes. 'All careers are bound to be disrupted at some point and therefore professionals entering the workplace should be aware that their journey is not going to be straightforward and predefined. There are many reasons for this, including the fact that technology will take over a lot of the tasks humans are currently doing. I would advise young professionals to broaden their horizons.'

According to him chartered accountants are lucky in that their qualification offers the foundation to pursue various positions. He further urges young professionals to seize the opportunity to work internationally when they can. In his view, it is important to work in different jurisdictions to experience diverse cultures and varied regulatory frameworks. This will enable harmonious engagements as offices become global, particularly in the post-COVID era, with more and more people working remotely.

'My three children are growing up in a vastly different environment from the one I grew up in. The world is a lot more competitive today and consequently there is more pressure to perform. You need to put in a lot more effort to get ahead and the coronavirus pandemic has accelerated that reality.'

One of the changes the pandemic has brought to our work style is the use of virtual meeting platforms, which has increased meeting schedules. 'Even when I'm on holiday, I get requested to join a call briefly, and then it lasts for hours. It can be problematic when meetings are disruptive rather than productive. A lot of meetings result from the regulatory environment as our engagements are geared to monitoring compliance. Be that as it may, they need to be as short as possible and have clear outcomes.'

In this he shares the sentiments of Stephen Covey, the bestselling author of *The 7 Habits of Highly Effective People*, who writes that he finds most meetings to be a waste of time because participants are often ill prepared.

Consequently, Riaan has learnt that it is important to be able to say no. That is the only way he can maintain a healthy work–life balance, which allows him to drop off his kids at school before work and make it to the gym in the evening. The ultimate highlight in his personal and professional life is making time to be a husband and a father.

INDEX

243

www.ingramcontent.com/pod-product-compliance
Lightning Source LLC
Chambersburg PA
CBHW071540200326
41519CB00021BB/6553